Studies in Consciousness / Russell Targ Editions

Some of the twentieth century's best texts on the scientific study of consciousness are out of print, hard to find, and unknown to most readers; yet they are still of great importance, their insights into human consciousness and its dynamics still valuable and vital. Hampton Roads Publishing Company—in partnership with physicist and consciousness research pioneer Russell Targ—is proud to bring some of these texts back into print, introducing classics in the fields of science and consciousness studies to a new generation of readers. Upcoming titles in the *Studies in Consciousness* series will cover such perennially exciting topics as telepathy, astral projection, the after-death survival of consciousness, psychic abilities, long-distance hypnosis, and more.

STUDIES IN CONSCIOUSNESS

Russell Targ Editions

Mind to Mind

René Warcollier

Preface by Ingo Swann

Interpretive Introduction by Russell Targ and Jane Katra, Ph. D.

HAMPTON ROADS
PUBLISHING COMPANY, INC.

Cover art by Anne L. Dunn

Hampton Roads Publishing Company, Inc.
1125 Stoney Ridge Road
Charlottesville, VA 22902

434-296-2772
fax: 434-296-5096
e-mail: hrpc@hrpub.com
www.hrpub.com

If you are unable to order this book from your local
bookseller, you may order directly from the publisher.
Call 1-800-766-8009, toll-free.

Library of Congress Catalog Card Number: 2001094010
ISBN 1-57174-311-1
10 9 8 7 6 5 4 3 2 1
Printed on acid-free paper in Canada

There is no metaphysical implication in the material I am presenting here. Our experiments are empirical and the data are presented as objective facts. I have made no compromise with my critical faculties. The parapsychologist does not wish to leave the impression that the mental image exists in objective space. It may be purely a fiction, but it is a scientifically necessary one. If it has reality, it is a psychological reality. Its existence lies in its function, which is never independent of the personalities involved. What is more, it is accessible to experimental investigation.

Human psychology is still in its infancy. There is much to be learned about the structure of the personality and about those forces to which we apply so glibly the term "human nature." Research in telepathy will have meaning in enlarging the horizons of psychological investigators. . . . At this point, it is appropriate to recall what McDougall had to say concerning the value of parapsychology. He said, "I believe that telepathy is very nearly established for all time among the facts recognised by Science. . . . If and when that result shall have been achieved, its importance for Science and Philosophy will far outweigh the sum of the achievements of all the psychological laboratories of the universities of two continents."

—from the Conclusion

CONTENTS

I PREFACE

This wonderful book was first published in 1948. Its gemlike contents were selected and translated from the greater bulk of René Warcollier's very impressive telepathy research in France.

Dr. Gardner Murphy, the distinguished psychologist and pioneer in parapsychology research, provided the timely introduction, which includes a biographical sketch of Warcollier. The book was brought out by Creative Edge Press, founded in 1941 by the famous and dynamic psychic-medium, Eileen J. Garrett, in order to publish her own book entitled *Telepathy.*

The 1948 edition could continue to stand on its own merits. But since many events and developments have taken place during the intervening decades, it is useful to partially reset Warcollier's seminal work into a larger, and now more inclusive, historical overview.

One reason for doing this is that when this book was first published, its astonishing revelations about the underlying processes of telepathy were widely acclaimed as a dramatic breakthrough. As it turns out, that breakthrough has not really been enlarged upon.

So the book represents a unique benchmark that has not yet been surpassed, leaving its revelations about telepathy sort of suspended in time, awaiting the minds of those who can recognize how to utilize and increase their dimensions.

Another reason to view the work in this context has to do with three concepts that are taken for granted today but which had not come into clear existence as of 1948: the concepts of models of the mind, information transfer, and signal-to-noise ratio.

These three important concepts have achieved broad recognition in science and technology, and their fundamentals can be applied to phenomena of the mind, telepathy, and other formats of psi as well. If they are factored backward into Warcollier's work, they enable a better and larger understanding of what is involved.

Still another reason has to do precisely with the models-of-the-mind situation. As a result of accumulating consciousness research since the 1950s, it has become possible to understand that people do develop basic frames of reference. These frames, in turn, have a great deal to do with how minds are set, and then with how reality is, or is not, viewed via these mindsets.

There is no doubt that researchers mind-model their research approaches, experimental methods, perspectives, and expectations within the scope of their own mindset's frames of reference. Different research approaches will, of course, end up producing different results. So when a given research model ends up producing extraordinary results and other research models do not, it seems the better part of valor to discover the precise frames of reference behind the successful research.

Such is the case with René Warcollier's overall research, and the parts of it that were presented as *Mind to Mind* in 1948.

That first edition, with Dr. Gardner Murphy's well-considered introduction, presented a relatively complete, if brief, picture of the Warcollier research. However, his basic frames of reference and fundamental research model were not pointed up or specifically elaborated upon.

This would not have been considered an omission in 1948. At the time, frames of reference were seen merely as subjective configurations that were not amenable to objective quantification. And so the then-developing scientific research model of American parapsychology was focusing on establishing objective quantification of psi, independent of any subjective frames of reference and mindsets of the researchers.

As it has turned out, however, objective quantification of telepathy has not really contributed very much to the understanding of what telepathy actually consists of beyond a collection of data. In high contrast, Warcollier's brief eighty-three pages of *Mind to Mind* reveal some several dozens of mind activities that take place within the overall phenomenon itself.

As will be found in the opening remarks of the text, Warcollier himself recognized and emphasized the fundamental importance of "frames of reference." Even though Warcollier's frames of reference, and resulting overall research model, were not included in the book, ample discussion of them is found throughout his French documents, where they are identified as constituting a crucial part of his research. So, what his basic frames consisted of is easily accessible and need not be drawn merely from latter-day supposition.

Warcollier was closely affiliated with the International Metapsychic Institute *(Institut Métapsychique International)* at Paris, serving as its treasurer from 1929–38, then as editor of its publication, *Revue Métapsychique,* from 1938–40, and as its president from 1951–62. At first take, it might be supposed that the Metapsychic Institute was merely the French equivalent of, for example, the British Society for Psychical Research and of the later formats of American parapsychology.

While all of those organizations investigated the same phenomena, each of them, in general, did so based on different frames of reference. Hence, the same phenomena were viewed differently, and this led into different conceptual pathways, many of which ended up in dead ends.

One of the difficulties in isolating what the different concepts consisted of has to do with the well-known fact that meanings of terms slip around over time. One such slippery term is "psychic." In more recent modern English, it became a sort of ambiguous generic term that could be used to refer to just about anything "paranormal."

An examination of the etymology of the term shows that its earliest meaning was more narrowly defined in both English and French. In English around 1642, and slightly earlier in French, "psychic" pertained to the mind, to the mental as distinguished from the physical.

It was not until the 1880s that the concepts of the psychical and psychic began to be utilized in English in ways that have remained familiar since: "Of or pertaining to phenomena and conditions which appear to lie outside the domain of physical law, and are therefore attributed by some to spiritual or hyperphysical agencies." (Oxford English Dictionary s.v. "psychical.") This new terminology led to an interest in psychical research of such phenomena and their conditions.

In French, the concept of the psychical remained more true to the earlier classical definition, "pertaining to the mind, to the mental as distinguished from the physical." (Cassell's French Dictionary s.v. "psychique.") And it is this classic sense that is basic to the meaning of the French term *métapsychique.*

That term was coined by the physiologist Dr. Charles Richet (1850–1935), one of France's most famous and most remembered scientists, who from 1887 to 1927 was professor of physiology at the Faculty of Medicine in Paris, and who received the 1913 Nobel Prize in Physiology and Medicine for his discovery of the anaphylaxis reaction.

By about 1887, Richet had concluded that there did exist, "in certain persons at certain times, a faculty of cognition which has no relation to our normal means of knowledge." (Encyclopedia of Occultism and Parapsychology s.v. "Richet.")

For this faculty he coined the term "cryptesthesia," and defined the faculty as "a hidden sensibility, a perception of things by a mechanism unknown to us of which we are cognizant only by its effects." (ibid. s.v. "cryptesthesia.")

Within his overall theory of cryptesthesia, Richet included clairvoyance, premonitions, monitions, psychometry, dowsing, and telepathy. He held that "telepathy as a hypothesis presupposes cryptesthesia as the reception of transmitted thought vibrations, and as such implies a new faculty." (ibid.) With this, Richet was referring to a hidden aspect of mind, perception, and thought, and this was made more precise when he coined the term "metapsychic" about 1903.

Among his many other posts and offices, he was in 1905 elected president of the Society for Psychical Research in London. In his inaugural address, he defined metapsychics as "a science dealing with mechanical or psychological phenomena due to forces which seem to be intelligent, or to unknown powers, latent in human intelligence."

For additional clarity, that definition can be refined to mean a science dealing with hitherto unknown and hidden mechanisms or forces that exist in human intelligence usually in a latent state, which seem to be intelligent of and in themselves, and which can function without the use of the five physical senses.

However the definition might be put, Richet was attributing to the metapsychical faculty some kind of intelligence autonomy that was independent of the five senses, but which nonetheless dealt in information and knowledge.

Thus, in French, the combination of *méta* and *psychique* sought to distinguish between the awake mind, closely linked to the physical senses, and a meta-mind, having perception, intelligence, and thought of its own, but which was hidden behind the mind as the average person knows it.

With specific reference to telepathy, it was then hypothesized that the telepathic faculty and its processes belonged to the hidden meta-mind, while the everyday mind, which was not conscious of the hidden mind, was only indirectly conscious of its effects.

Here, then, is a crucial distinction between the American parapsychology mindset as formatted during the 1930s and the earlier French metapsychical mindset that was formatted before World War I.

The American mindset sought to scientifically establish what could be quantified of the physical aspects of psychical phenomena, while the earlier French mindset, which characterized Warcollier's basic frames of reference, wanted to scientifically isolate and examine the qualitative processes of the hidden meta-mind. Involved in this distinction, and clearly so, are the pathways of two different kinds of basic, and largely opposite, frames of reference.

In 1918, Richet was instrumental in the founding of the International Metapsychic Institute in Paris, which attracted the interest of large numbers of eminent personalities in science, literature, and philosophy from many nations. Although there was some thirty-one years age difference between them, the close affiliation of Warcollier and Richet began before World War I and lasted until Richet's death in 1935.

Their collaboration within the contexts of the metapsychic mind-model produced high quality results, especially with regard to isolating patterns within telepathic activity *(les dessins télépathique).*

Between 1951 and 1962, the year of his own death, Warcollier was the president of the Metapsychic Institute. Between 1924 and 1962, the Institute published fifty-six of Warcollier's papers; forty-eight of these came out after Richet's death. Among these papers were: "A contribution to the study of mental imagery" (1948); "Psychic space-time" (1949); "Qualitative evidence of telepathy" (1957); and "Mental contagion within group telepathy" (1962).

Upon reading the foregoing, it becomes quite clear that Warcollier's model for telepathy was not exactly based in the mind-to-mind idea, but in the meta-mind to meta-mind concept. In other words, it is not the daily, average, awake, conscious mind that has telepathic faculties. Rather, those faculties belong to the meta-minds of the individuals involved, the processes of which are "hidden" from the awake conscious mind. As Warcollier indicated, the awake conscious mind becomes aware of those processes only by experiencing their effects.

In 1948, American parapsychologists would have had trouble giving legitimacy to the idea of a hidden meta-mind, and so it is understandable why more extensive discussion of it was avoided back then. But now, more than fifty years later, the meta-mind concept is at least partially vindicated.

Researchers of brain-information processing now understand that the brain's sensing systems are, in a meta- kind of way, non-consciously processing enormous amounts of information in some kind of mysterious, perhaps electronic, form.

But on average, only about 24 percent or less of the larger information whole is downloaded into the awake mind. This 24 percent generally involves only what fits into an individual's frames of reference, which are being utilized to establish reality for the individual. This percentile situation brings new credence not only to the concept of Warcollier's meta-mind, but to the recent idea of the multidimensional consciousness as well.

In addition to stating that telepathy is a meta-mind function, Warcollier defined telepathy as including "the communication of emotions, ideas, mental images, sensations, or words from one individual to another without the help of the [physical] senses."

He also understood that telepathic faculties were involved with information processing and information transfer from sender to receiver(s). But not directly so, in that the transmission is beset with distortions, confusions, mental overlays, and time lags.

The basic reason for these difficulties is that "Images sent are [somehow] broken apart in meta-psychic time/space and [somehow] reassembled by the receiver." And so all sorts of ambient mental and other phenomena can get in the way of clear and perfect reassembling.

Although the term signal-to-noise ratio was early encountered as a complication in radio broadcasting, it did not come into its own in other disciplines until the 1950s, when it took on importance as a factor within general information theory and information transfer processes. "Signal," of course, refers to information being sent from one source to a receiver, while "noise" refers to what distorts, dilutes, or disturbs clear reception at the receiving end. Noise can also be referred to as "static" which blocks clear reception of the signal.

Mind to Mind is not actually a discourse on telepathy itself or whether it actually exists. Rather, it is a treatise on the clarity of telepathic signals and what dilutes or distorts clear reassembling in the mind and meta-mind of the receiver. In other words, Warcollier's work precisely foreshadowed the signal-to-noise problems within the telepathy-sending and -receiving processes.

One of the most interesting aspects of Warcollier's work, however, has to do with why he and his colleagues were so successful in isolating about sixty subtle telepathy signal noise aspects that are inherent in the larger undifferentiated whole of the phenomenon.

That reason is very briefly mentioned, almost as an aside, in Warcollier's text. And so its importance might be missed today as it was in the past.

Fundamentally speaking, telepathy is a problem within the contexts of information transfer. If information transfer from one meta-mind to another is considered, one needs to know not only what was sent versus what was received, but also the degree and variations of success or failure.

To this end, Warcollier elected to utilize some simple and some complex picture drawings for his experiments. Thus, the sender could try to send a prepared picture drawing, while the receiver, not knowing anything about the drawing except that it was one, then made a picture drawing of what was received.

This technique allowed factors within the reassembling processes to be studied and compared. With a sufficient number of experimental results in hand, it became possible to isolate, compare, and categorize various subtle and remarkable subsidiary processes within the larger telepathy whole.

It is the comparing and categorizing of telepathy signals and noise that constitutes the substantive backbone of this gemlike and precious book—precious not only because Warcollier's work is clearly suggestive that a mind-dynamic telepathy technology could be possible, but that his work could be used as a seminal basis for such a technology.

Ingo Swann, New York, 2001

Note: *Mind to Mind* should be read in conjunction with *Mental Radio,* and *Thoughts Through Space,* also reprinted in this marvelous series called Classics in Consciousness. Discussions regarding how much brain-information is processed and how little of it downloads into awake consciousness can be found in *The User Illusion: Cutting Consciousness Down to Size* by Tor Norretranders, Penguin Books, 1998.

I INTERPRETIVE INTRODUCTION

Since ancient times, spiritual teachers have described paths and practices that a person could follow to achieve health, happiness, and peace of mind. Considerable recent research has indicated that any sort of spiritual practice is likely to improve one's prognosis for recovering from a serious illness. Many of these approaches to spirituality involve learning to quiet the mind rather than adhering to a prescribed religious belief. These meditative paths include the mystic branches of Buddhism, Hinduism, and Christianity; Kabalistic Judaism; Sufism; and many others. What is hinted at in the subtext of these teachings is that as one learns to quiet his or her mind, one is likely to encounter psychic-seeming experiences or perceptions. For example, in The Sutras of Patanjali, the Hindu master tells us that on the way to transcendence we may experience all sorts of amazing visions, such as the ability to see into the distance, or into the future, and to diagnose illnesses and to cure them. However, we are told not to get attached to these psychic abilities—they are mere phenomena standing as stumbling blocks on the path to enlightenment. In this article, we describe the laboratory evidence for some of these remarkable phenomena and their implications for science, mental health, and peace of mind. (Altern. Ther. Health Med. 2001;7(3):143-149)

What do the spiritual healer, the mystic, and the scientist all have in common? The answer is that they are all in touch with their interconnected and nonlocal mind. In my (R. T.'s) work with remote viewing research at Stanford Research Institute, we observed the inflow of information that is the hallmark of psychic perception. We also saw an outflow of intention that plays a part in facilitating distant healing. Our purpose here is to show that the inflow and the outflow reside on either side of the quiet mind, and that self-awareness can arise between these two flows. We have also noticed that narrowly focusing on phenomena, and the seeming omniscience available from extrasensory perception (ESP), may be just a trap that prevents us from discovering who we really are and what we should be doing. However, as my coauthor Jane Katra and I describe in *The Heart of the Mind,*[1] we are confident that whenever any one person demonstrates an ability beyond the ordinary, it can be seen as an inspiration to the rest of us, as an indication of an immense and still largely undeveloped human potential.

The scientific and spiritual implications of psychic abilities illuminate our observation that we live in a profoundly interconnected world. The most exciting research in quantum physics today is the investigation of what physicist David Bohm calls "quantum-interconnectedness," or nonlocal correlations.[2] It has been demonstrated repeatedly in laboratories around the world that quanta of light that are sent off in opposite directions at light speed maintain their connection to one another, and that each little photon is affected by what happens to its twin, many kilometers away.[3-5] This surprising coherence between distant entities is called nonlocality. In writing on the philosophical implications of nonlocality, physicist Henry Stapp of the University of California, Berkeley, says that these quantum connections could be the "most profound discovery in all of science."[6]

Psychic abilities and remote viewing are demonstrations of our personal experience with such nonlocal connection in consciousness. Mind-to-mind connections that transcend our ordinary understanding of space and time give us expanded awareness, which is entirely consistent with life in a nonlocal world. This connection is what physicists mean by nonlocality. To the healer, it gives rise to what Larry Dossey[7] refers to in his book *Reinventing Medicine* as Era III healing of a distant patient through the intentionality of the healer. Our knowledge of these remarkable abilities allows us to awaken each morning in wonder at the fact that our expanded awareness is not limited by either time or space. And it should have become clear to us by now that although we reside in bodies, there is more to us than skin and bones. Our quiet moments of self-inquiry can reveal what that "more" is.

Remote Viewing

Stanford Research Institute (SRI) conducted investigations into the human mind's capacity for expanded awareness, also called remote viewing, in which people are able to envision distant places and future events and activities. For two decades, SRI's research was supported by the Central Intelligence Agency

(CIA) and other government agencies. I was cofounder of this once secret program, which began in 1972. Our task was to learn to understand psychic abilities and to use these abilities to gather information about the Soviet Union during the Cold War. We have found from years of experience that people can quickly learn to do remote viewing and can frequently incorporate this direct knowing of the world—both present and future—into their lives.

Considering that these phenomena are thought in many circles not to exist, we certainly know a great deal about how to increase and decrease ESP's accuracy and reliability. Remote viewers can often contact, experience, and describe a hidden object, or a remote natural or architectural site, on the basis of the presence of a cooperative person at the distant location, or when given geographical coordinates or some other target demarcation, which we call an address. Shape, form, and color are described much more reliably than the target's name, function, or other analytical information. In addition to vivid visual imagery, viewers sometimes describe associated feelings, sounds, smells, and even electrical or magnetic fields.

Blueprint accuracy occasionally has been achieved in these double-blind experiments, and reliability in a series has been as high as eighty percent. For example, the authors recently achieved eleven hits out of twelve trials in such a series.[8] With practice, people become increasingly able to separate out the psychic signal from the mental noise of memory, analysis, and imagination. Targets and target details as small as one millimeter can be sensed. Again and again we have seen that the accuracy and resolution of remote viewing targets are not sensitive to variations in distance. In 1984 I organized a pair of successful ten-thousand-mile remote viewing experiments between Moscow and San Francisco with famed Russian healer Djuna Davitashvili. Djuna's task was to describe where our colleague would be hiding in San Francisco. She had to focus her attention ten thousand miles to the west and two hours into the future to describe his location correctly. These experiments were performed under the auspices and control of the USSR Academy of Sciences.

Ten years earlier, in 1974, my colleague Hal Puthoff and I carried out a demonstration of psychic abilities for the CIA in which Pat Price, a retired police commissioner, described the inside and outside of a secret Soviet weapons laboratory in the far reaches of Siberia with only the geographical coordinates of latitude and longitude for reference (i.e., with no on-site cooperation). This trial was such a stunning success that we were forced to undergo a formal congressional investigation to determine whether there had been a breach in national security. Of course, no such breach was ever found, and we were supported by the government for another fifteen years. As I sat with Price in these experiments at SRI, he made a sketch (Figure 1) to illustrate his mental impressions of a giant gantry crane that he psychically "saw" rolling back and forth over a building at the target site.

Data from our formal and controlled SRI investigations were highly statistically significant (thousands of times greater than chance expectation), and have been published in the world's most prestigious journals, including *Nature, Proceedings of the Institute of Electrical and Electronics Engineers (IEEE),* and *Proceedings of the American Association for the Advancement of Science (AAAS).*[9-11] The twenty years of remote viewing research conducted for the CIA is outlined in *Miracles of Mind: Exploring Nonlocal Consciousness and Spiritual Healing,* coauthored by Russell Targ and Jane Katra.[12]

One day, while we were working with Pat Price, he did not arrive for the scheduled experiment. So, in the spirit of "the show must go on," I spontaneously decided to undertake the remote viewing myself. Before that, I had been only an interviewer and facilitator for such trials. In this series, we were trying to describe the day-to-day activities of Hal Puthoff as he traveled through Colombia, South America. We would not receive any feedback until he returned, and I therefore had no clues at all as to what he was doing. I closed my eyes and immediately had an image of an island airport. The surprisingly accurate sketch I drew is shown in Figure 2. What we learned from this trial is that even a scientist can be psychic, when the necessity level is high enough.

Recent research in areas as different as distant healing and quantum physics are in alignment with the oldest spiritual teachings of the sages of India, who taught that "separation is an illusion." This concept suggests that there is no distance for consciousness, and that we have an intuitive inner knowledge of time and space. In fact, we now know that information from the future regularly filters into our dreams—one could fairly say that these precognitive dreams indicate that the future affects our past. In other words, our dream tonight may be caused by an event that we will experience at a later time, strongly violating our ordinary understanding of causality. In our work together as physicist and spiritual healer, we have been exploring how our mind's ability to transcend the limits of space and time is linked to our now-documented capacity for distant healing.

We do not yet know the physics underlying psychic abilities. But researchers in the field of parapsychology agree on the undeniable observation that it is no more difficult to psychically describe a picture or an event in the near future than it is to describe such a target in the present, when it is hidden from view.[13]

A

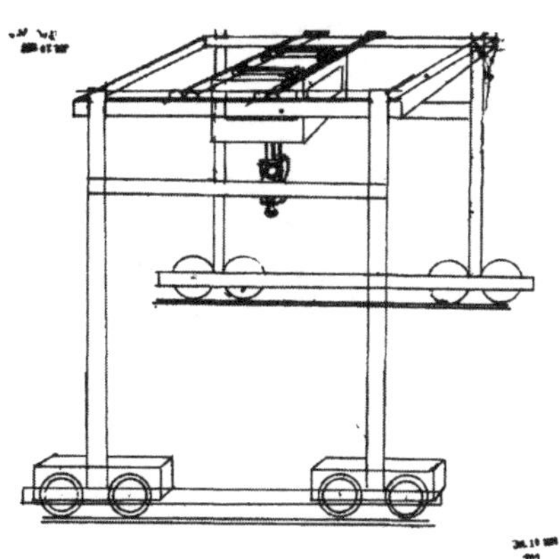

FIGURE 1 On the top, in part A is Pat Price's drawing of his psychic impressions of a gantry crane at the secret Soviet research and development site at Semipalatinsk, showing remarkable similarity to a later Central Intelligence Agency (CIA) drawing based on satellite photography shown on the bottom. Note. For example, that both cranes have eight wheels. In part B a CIA artist's tracing of a satellite photograph of the Semipalatinsk target site is pictured. Such tracings were made by the CIA to conceal the accuracy of detail of satellite photography at that time.

It is as though our bodies reside in the familiar four-dimensional geometry of Einstein's space-time, while our consciousness has access to another aspect of this geometry that allows us to find a mental path of zero distance to seemingly distant locations. This is how a physicist expresses such an idea, while mystics for the past three millennia tell us from their experience that "separation is an illusion—and we are all one in spirit, or consciousness." From experimentation

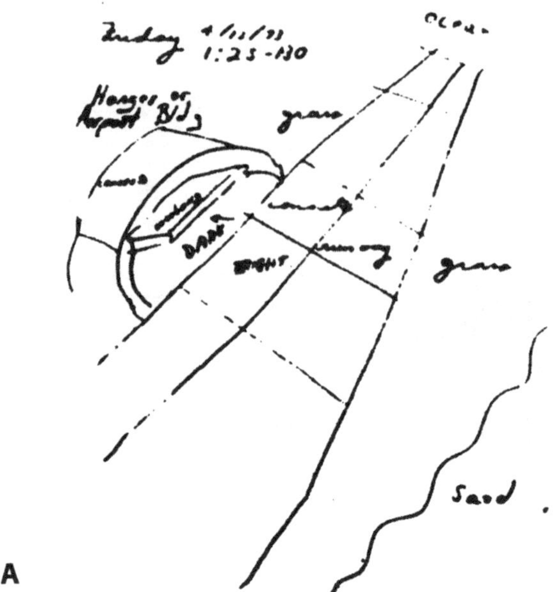

SA-2613-20H

FIGURE 2 On the top (A) is a sketch produced by physicist Russell Targ when he spontaneously took the role of remote viewer in the absence of psychic Pat Price. On the bottom (B) is a photograph showing the target, which was an airport on an island off San Andres, Colombia. Targ correctly saw that there was an "[o]cean at the end of a runway."

in many laboratories, it is clear that we significantly misapprehend the physical nature of the space-time in which we reside. It is this knowledge, together with our experience, that drives our passion to understand and learn more about the universe and the transformational opportunities offered us.

Joseph Campbell is famous for teaching that our lives are fulfilled only when we "follow our bliss." For Thomas Aquinas, this passion was pursued through conscious reasoning. He wrote that "[t]he ultimate human felicity is found in the operation of the intellect, since no desire carries us to such heights as the desire to understand the truth. Indeed all our desires for pleasure or for other things can be satisfied, but the desire to understand does not rest until it reaches God."[14] However, those who truly understand the truth of God tell us that God cannot be understood, only experienced.

Distant Mental Influence of Living Systems

More than thirty years of investigations clearly show that one person's thoughts can affect the physiological functioning of another distant person. We do not yet understand the causal mechanism involved, but the results are indisputable, and have obvious implications for our ability to facilitate healing in others. This healing, whether in the laboratory or in a clinical setting, is considered to be nonlocal, because the efficacy of the healing or mental influence is independent of distance. We take for granted the calming effects that a mother's gentle cooing has on her distressed infant, not really thinking about the effects of her soothing intentions. How do we know that our thoughts affect others? A significant body of research now exists demonstrating that one person's focused intentions can directly influence the physiological processes of someone far away. "Do unto others as you would have them do unto you" takes on new meaning when you realize we are all truly connected, as the following research studies show.

Exciting experiments in the area of distant mental influence of living systems (DMILS) have been carried out by psychologist William Braud at the Institute of Transpersonal Psychology in Palo Alto, California, and anthropologist Marilyn Schlitz, research director at the Institute of Noetic Sciences in Novato, California.[15,16] They have repeatedly shown that if a person simply attends fully to a distant person whose physiological activity is being monitored, he or she (acting as a sender) can influence the distant person's autonomic galvanic skin responses. In four separate experiments involving seventy-eight sessions, one person staring intently at a closed-circuit television monitor image of a distant participant influenced the remote person's electrodermal (galvanic skin) responses. In these cases, no techniques of intentional focusing or mental imaging were used by the influencer. He or she simply stared at the "staree's" image on the video screen during the thirty-second trials that were randomly interspersed with control periods.

In these studies, Braud and Schlitz discovered something even more interesting than this telepathically induced effect on our unconscious system: they found that the most anxious and introverted people being stared at had the greatest magnitudes of unconscious electrodermal responses. In other words, shy and introverted people reacted with significantly more stress to being stared at than did sociable and extroverted people. Quiet introverts may possess, or have developed, a sensitivity of consciousness that others are less aware of. This experiment gives scientific validation to the common human experience of feeling stared at and turning around to find that someone is, indeed, staring at you.

We are all familiar with the idea of premonition, in which one has an intuitive apprehension of something about to happen in the future—usually something "bad." There is also the experience of presentiment, wherein one has an inner sensation—a gut feeling—that something strange is about to occur. An example would be when you suddenly stop on your walk down the street because you feel "uneasy," only to have a flower pot fall off a window ledge and land at your feet instead of on your head. That, of course, would be a useful presentiment.

In the laboratory, we know that showing a frightening picture to a person produces a significant change in that person's physiology. His or her blood pressure, heart rate, and skin resistance all change. This fight-or-flight reaction is called an "orienting response." Researcher Dean Radin, at the Institute of Noetic Studies in Petaluma, California, has shown in his work that this orienting response is also observed in a person's physiology a few seconds before the person views the scary picture. Although electromagnetic theory would describe this as an advanced wave, we believe this information arises directly from timeless nonlocal consciousness.

In balanced, double-blind experiments, Radin has demonstrated that just before viewing scenes of violence or sexuality, one's body apparently reacts to defend itself against the oncoming insult or surprise. However, such strong anticipatory shock reactions did not precede the viewing of a picture of a wastebasket or a flower garden. Of course, fear is much easier to measure physiologically than is bliss. Here, it seems, a person's direct physical perception of the shocking picture, when it occurs, causes him or her to have a unique physical response five seconds earlier. Your future is affecting your past. These intriguing experiments are also described in Radin's comprehensive book, *The Conscious Universe.*[17]

Distant Healing

From the dawn of history, certain individuals have been recognized as possessing special healing gifts. The pharaohs of ancient Egypt viewed healers as revered advisers. In fact, healers founded the world's great religions: Gautama Buddha, Jesus of Nazareth, and the prophet Muhammad all were gifted healers. The earliest Christians were primarily a healing community, and centuries before Jesus the Hebrew prophets Elijah, Elisha, and Isaiah were acknowledged healers. Moses is said to have healed many Israelites from serpent bites.

Medicine men and healing shamans throughout Africa, Asia, and the Americas held some of the most esteemed positions in their tribes. By contrast, the progression of Western thought has largely ignored the broad range of mind-to-mind healing that has worked in other cultures. With our reverence for Humanism and Reason, we have much to relearn about the role of consciousness in healing. Only now are we realizing the power of the mind to heal through the scientific method. In recent years, a number of pioneering experiments have explored the role one person's consciousness may have on another person's health.

In his 1993 book *Healing Research,*[18] psychiatrist Daniel J. Benor, M.D., examined more than one hundred and fifty controlled studies from around the world. He reviewed psychic, mental, and spiritual healing experiments done on a variety of living organisms, including enzymes, cell cultures, bacteria, yeasts, plants, animals, and humans. More than half of the studies demonstrated significant healing.[18]

An important study by Fred Sicher, Elisabeth Targ, and associates describing healing research done at California Pacific Medical Center was published in the December 1998 issue of the *Western Medical Journal.*[19] The article describes the positive therapeutic effects of distant healing or intentionality on men with advanced AIDS.

In this mainstream medical journal, the researchers defined nonlocal or distant healing as an act of "mentation intended to benefit another person's physical and/or emotional well-being at a distance," adding that "[i]t has been found in some form in nearly every culture since prehistoric time." Their research hypothesized that an intensive ten-week distant healing intervention by experienced healers located around the United States would benefit the medical outcomes for a population of patients with advanced AIDS in the San Francisco area.

The researchers performed two separate, randomized, double-blind studies: a pilot study involving twenty male subjects stratified by number of AIDS-defining illnesses, and a replication study of forty men carefully matched into pairs by age, T-cell count, and number of AIDS-defining illnesses. The participants' conditions were assessed by psychometric testing and blood testing at enrollment, after the distant healing intervention, and six months later, when physicians reviewed their medical charts.

In the pilot study, four of the ten control subjects died, whereas all of subjects in the treatment group survived. But this result was possibly confounded by unequal age distributions in the two groups. In the replication study, men with AIDS were again recruited from the San Francisco Bay Area. They were told that they had a fifty-fifty chance of being in the treatment group or the control group. All subjects were pair-matched for age, CD4 count, and AIDS-defining diseases. Forty distant healers from all parts of the country took part in the study. Each of them had more than five years' experience in a particular form of healing. They were from Christian, Jewish, Buddhist, Native American, and shamanic traditions, in addition to secular "bioenergetic" schools.

Each subject in the healing group was treated by a total of ten different healers on a rotating healing schedule. Healers were asked to work on their assigned subject for approximately one hour per day for six consecutive days, with instructions to "direct an intention of health and well-being" to the subject to whom they were attending. None of the forty subjects in the study ever met the healers, nor did they or the experimenters know into which group anyone had been randomized.

By the midpoint of the study, neither group of participants was able to guess at better than chance levels whether they were in the healing condition. However, by the end of the study, subjects in the healing group had many fewer opportunistic illnesses, allowing the healing group to identify itself—with significant odds against chance. Because all of the patients were being treated with triple-drug therapy, no deaths occurred in either group. The treatment group experienced significantly better medical and quality-of-life outcomes (odds of 100:1) on many quantitative measures, including fewer outpatient doctor visits (185 vs 260); fewer days of hospitalization (10 vs 68); less severe illnesses acquired during the study, as measured by illness severity scores (16 vs 43); and significantly less emotional distress. Dr Targ concludes:

"Decreased hospital visits, fewer severe new diseases, and greatly improved subjective health supports the hypothesis of positive therapeutic effects of distant healing."

The editor of the journal introduced the paper with these thoughts: "The paper published below is meant to advance science and debate. It has been reviewed, revised, and re-reviewed by nationally known experts in biostatistics, and complementary medicine. . . . We have chosen to publish this provocative paper to stimulate other studies of distant healing, and other complementary practices and agents. It is time for more light, less dark, less heat."

Two other studies of distant healing have been published in prestigious medical journals. In 1988, Randolph C. Byrd, MD, published a successful double-blind demonstration of distant healing in the *Southern Medical Journal.* The study involved 393 of his cardiac patients at San Francisco General Hospital.[20] And, in 1999, cardiologist William Harris and associates of the University of Missouri in Kansas City published a similar successful study with 990 heart patients. That paper appeared in the *Archives of Internal Medicine.*[21]

All three clinical experiments departed significantly from chance expectation. But the work of Sicher and Targ[19] required less than one tenth the number of patients to achieve this significance. We attribute this greater effect size ($Z/N^{1/2}$) to the fact that Sicher and Targ worked with healers who each had more than five years of healing experience, whereas the others worked with well intentioned but much less experienced people. A detailed analysis of twenty-three clinical studies of intercessory prayer and distant healing recently was published by John Astin and colleagues in the *Annals of Internal Medicine.*[22] An examination of sixteen studies that they determined were adequately double-blinded showed an effect size of 0.4 for 2,139 patients ($P<.001$). In addition, two excellent analyses of distant intentionality and distant healing studies have been published in *Alternative Therapies* by pioneering researchers Marilyn Schlitz and William Braud[23] and psychiatrist Elisabeth Targ.[24]

Mindful of the nonlocal nature of our universe, Braud[25] recently conjectured that our healing intentions may achieve their goal by reaching backward in time to affect critical "seed moments" in alternate future pathways of the development of the illness. Braud suggests that these early moments may be more labile and hence more susceptible avenues of change in intercessory distant healing. This idea of backward causation is like the previously described experience of precognitive dreams, in which our dream in the night is ostensibly "caused" by the confirmatory experience that we typically have the next day. Modern physics seems to indicate that we live in a nonlocal spider web of space and time, where *both* the future and the past are tugging on the present.

Scientists do not yet clearly understand how the mind-stuff of one's own intentions results in the contractions of one's muscles. It remains a mystery how the invisible mind moves the physical body. But we do know that it is more powerful than we previously thought. Twentieth-century science has documented that our thoughts affect others; that we are all interconnected through our consciousness. We are not even alone in experiencing the effects of our own thoughts!

We are actually already hooked up to the psychic Internet—Jung's "collective unconscious." But the users are primarily those who have learned to stop their thoughts and rest their attention. They are tuning in to access and affect the exchange of information.

Why Would a Scientist Pray?

Today, many of us are searching for a comprehensible spirituality, one in which experience takes primacy over religious belief. We need not believe or take on faith anything about the existence of universal spirit, because the experience of God is a testable hypothesis, as we describe next. However, philosophical proof is not our purpose; rather, we have become aware that this experience is available to anyone seeking a spiritual life who also desires to remain a critical and discerning participant in the twenty-first century. We can include God in our lives without giving up our minds, if we can transcend our usual analytical thoughts and learn to become mindful. A scientist might pray or search for "the peace which passes understanding" as a way to experience the truth without conscious thought.

In his 1939 essay "Science and Religion," Albert Einstein[26] suggested that we each have the potential for a greater awareness of truth than analysis alone can offer: "Objective knowledge provides us with powerful instruments for the achievements of certain ends. But, the ultimate goal itself, and the longing to reach it, must come from another source."

Wisdom teachers throughout history have shown that the experience of God is possible without belonging to a church or following a religion, as long as one's basic motive is to discover truth. Herbert Benson[27] recently proposed that we—our bodies and our brains—are "hard-wired for God." By this he means that throughout the past twenty-five hundred years—from Buddha, Jesus, and the *Ba'al Shem Tov* (Israel ben Eliezer, the founder of Hasidic Judaism), to such poets as Rumi, Blake, and Emerson—mystics have shared a common experience that is actually available to us all. In the mystic paths, the *experience* of God is celebrated rather than the belief in God or the religious ritual. The Sufi poet Rumi shared his thoughts that arose after experiencing his own divinity:

> All day I think about it, then at night I say it.
> Where did I come from, and what am I supposed to be doing?
> I have no idea.
> My soul is from elsewhere, I'm sure of that,
> And I intend to end up there.[28]

Whenever we sit peacefully and quiet our mind, we have an opportunity to experience an oceanic connection with something outside our separate self. To many, that connection is experienced as an overpowering feeling of love, and it may well constitute part of our evolutionary process as a species.

This feeling of universal love, without any particular object, is often associated with the realization that we reside within an extended community of spirit enveloping all living beings. Such feelings of unbounded interconnected consciousness have been described by many as an experience of God. The gift of a quiet mind allows us to understand what it means to be in love, like being immersed in loving syrup, as contrasted with being in love with another person. It is possible to reside in love (or gratitude) as a way of life. This experience is the source of the often heard expression that "God is love," which in an ordinary context is easily dismissed as a simple cliché, or worse, as incomprehensible.

These oceanic, loving, peaceful experiences are examples of the compelling feeling of "oneness" that mystics have been urging us to explore for millennia. Jesus called this state of awareness "the peace that passes all understanding," and a "kingdom which is not of this world." Hindus call it "bliss," or *ananda.* And Buddha called it a state of "no-mind," meaning the absence of thoughts disrupting awareness of indivisible unity.

The Path of Self-Inquiry

Early in the twentieth century, two of the world's greatest logicians, Ludwig Wittgenstein and Alfred Ayer, attempted to describe the physics and metaphysics of what can be known about reality. These Logical Positivists proclaimed that nothing meaningful could be said about God, because no experiment could be designed to either prove or disprove (verify or falsify) whatever one might say. But, by the end of their lives, both Wittgenstein and Ayer were willing to seriously examine the idea that the experience of mystics might actually be considered data—something observable in an experiment. In fact, in Wittgenstein's last book, *On Certainty,* he gave primacy to experience over theory. This preeminent logician tells us: "The solution to the riddle of life in space and time lies outside space and time."[29]

For thousands of years, various wisdom teachers have presented a worldview to those who will listen. They have described a "sit down and be quiet" practice that is available for all to observe and experience. They then invite us to examine our experience and see if it corresponds to their teaching. Ultimately, this seems like an acceptably scientific, empirical approach to spirituality.

Thirty years ago, national U.S. magazines proclaimed on their covers that "God is dead." Today, we would say that God is neither alive nor dead, but rather manifesting as activity in consciousness—transcending and transforming one's ordinary awareness. God is an active personal experience rather than a distant entity in the sky. Our five familiar senses bring us data of the material world, while filtering out and limiting our exposure to the wider, transcendent world of active awareness available to the quiet mind. The direction of our attention is the most powerful tool we have to transform our lives.

After centuries of academic bombast, we are finally coming to recognize how tentative so-called scientific "truth" really is. In a scientific world increasingly governed by so-called laws of "indeterminacy" (Werner Heisenberg) and "nonlocality" (John Bell) in physics, and "incompleteness" (Kurt Gödel) in mathematics, we are beginning to find room for the experience of God.

Philosopher Ken Wilber makes this point with great force in his book *Quantum Questions.*[30] He asserts convincingly that whereas physics will never explain spirituality, the spiritual realms may be explored by the scientific method: "The preposterous claim that all religious experience is private and noncommunicable is stopped dead by, to give only one example, the transmission of the Buddha's enlightenment all the way down to present-day Buddhist masters (which allows it to be experienced and discussed today)."[30]

Wilber describes three different but equally valid avenues of scientific empiricism: the eye of the flesh, which informs us about the world of our senses; the eye of the mind, which allows us access to mathematics, ideas, and logic; and the eye of contemplation, which is our window to the world of spiritual experience. None of these approaches suggest that we must embrace any body of dogma, or that we need to integrate Santa Claus into a scientific view of the modern world. They do, however, invite us to look beyond our thinking mind to discover who we are.

Although we cannot always control the events around us, we do have power over how we experience those events. At any moment, we can individually and collectively affect the course of our lives by choosing to direct our attention to the aspect of ourselves that is aware—and through the practice of self-inquiry, to awareness itself. Indian saint Ramana Maharshi[31] taught that we can ask, "Who is aware?" and then, "Who wants to know?" The choice of where we put our attention is ultimately our most powerful freedom. Our choice of attitude and focus affects not only our own perceptions and experiences, but also the experiences and behaviors of others.

We conclude that the scientific and spiritual implications of psychic abilities are evident in the continually unfolding mystery of the space-time in which we live. And a quiet mind has the opportunity for experiencing itself as love that is timeless, eternal, and unseparated by our bodies.

Russell Targ and Jane Katra, Ph.D.

References

1. Katra J, Targ R. *The Heart of the Mind: How to Experience God Without Belief.* Novato, Calif: New World Library; 1999.
2. Bohm D, Hiley B. *The Undivided Universe.* London, England: Routledge; 1993.
3. Freedman S, Clauser J. Experimental test of local hidden variable theories. *Phys Rev Lett.* 1972; 28:934-941.
4. Aspect A, et al. Experimental tests of Bell's inequality using time-varying analyzers. *Phys Rev Lett.* 1992; 49:1804-1907.
5. Tittel W, Brendel J, Zbinden H, Gisin N. Violation of Bell inequalities by photons more than 10 km apart. *Phys Rev Lett.* 1998; 81:3563-3566.
6. Kafatos M, Nadeau R. *The Conscious Universe: Parts and Wholes in Physical Reality.* New York, NY: Springer Verlag; 2000.
7. Dossey L. *Reinventing Medicine.* San Francisco, Calif: Harper; 1999.
8. Targ R, Katra J, Brown D, Wiegand D. Viewing the future: a pilot study with an error-detecting protocol. *J Sci Exploration.* 1995; 9:367-380.
9. Puthoff HE, Targ R. A perceptual channel for information transfer over kilometer distances: historical perspective and recent research. *Proc IEEE.* 1976; 64:329-254.
10. Targ R, Puthoff H. Information transfer under conditions of sensory shielding. *Nature.* 1975; 251:602-607.
11. Puthoff HE, Targ R, May EC. Experimental psi research: implication for physics. In: *AAAS Proceedings of the 1979 Symposium on the Role of Consciousness in the Physical World.* Washington, DC: American Association for the Advancement of Science; 1981.

12. Targ R, Katra J. *Miracles of Mind: Exploring Nonlocal Consciousness and Spiritual Healing.* Novato, Calif: New World Library; 1998.
13. Dunne BJ, Jahn RG, Nelson RD. *Precognitive Remote Perception.* Princeton, NJ: Princeton Engineering Anomalies Research Laboratory; 1983.
14. Aquinas T. Cited in: Mitchell S. *Meetings With the Archangel: A Comedy of the Spirit.* New York, NY: Harper Perennial Library; 1999.
15. Schlitz M, LaBerge S. Covert observation increases skin conductance in subjects unaware of when they are being observed: a replication. *J Parapsychology.* September 1997:185-196.
16. Braud W, Schlitz M. Psychokinetic influence on electro-dermal activity. *J Parapsychology.* 1983; 47:95-119.
17. Radin D. *The Conscious Universe.* San Francisco, Calif: Harper Collins; 1997.
18. Benor DJ. *Healing Research.* Vol 1. Munich, Germany: Helix Verlag; 1992.
19. Sicher F, Targ E, Moore D, Smith H. A randomized double-blind study of the effect of distant healing in a population with advanced AIDS. *West J Med.* 1998; 169:356-363.
20. Byrd RC. Positive therapeutic effects of intercessory prayer in a coronary care unit population. *South Med J.* 1988; 81:826-829.
21. Harris WS, Gowda M, Kolb JW, et al. A randomized, controlled trial of the effects of remote intercessory prayer on outcomes in patients admitted to the coronary care unit. *Arch Intern Med.* 1999; 159:2273-2278.
22. Astin JA, Harkness E, Ernst E. The efficacy of 'distant healing': a systematic review of randomized trials. *Ann Intern Med.* 2000; 132:903-910.
23. Schlitz M, Braud W. Distant intentionality and healing: assessing the evidence. *Altern Ther Health Med.* 1997; 3(6):62-73.
24. Targ E. Evaluating distant healing: a research review. *Altern Ther Health Med.* 1977; 3(6):74-78.
25. Braud W. Wellness implications of retroactive intentional influence: exploring an outrageous hypothesis. *Altern Ther Health Med.* 2000; 6:37-48.
26. Einstein A. *Out of My Later Years.* Secaucus, NJ: The Citadel Press; 1956.
27. Benson H. *Timeless Healing: The Power and Biology of Belief.* New York, NY: Simon & Schuster; 1997.
28. Barks C. *The Illuminated Rumi.* New York, NY: Broadway Books; 1997.
29. Wittgenstein L. *Tractatus-logico Philosophicus.* London, England: Routledge; 1974.
30. Wilber K. *Quantum Questions: Mystical Writings of the World's Great Physicists.* Boston, Mass: Shambhala; 1984.
31. Maharshi R. *Talks With Ramana Maharshi: On Realizing Abiding Peace and Happiness.* Carlsbad, Calif: Inner Directions Publishing; 2000.

I FOREWORD

THE CONTENTS of this book were originally conceived as a lecture, delivered at the Sorbonne in June of 1946, under the title, *A Contribution to the Study of Mental Imagery Through Telepathic Drawing*. The author, René Warcollier, sought to present some generalizations from hundreds of experiments in telepathy and forty years of research in parapsychology.

What one will discover, however, is more than a description of what happens when drawings are used as messages in telepathic communication. Here is a study of pictorial images typical of the varieties of mental imagery common to mankind. These are the images found in literature, in music, and in other expressions of creative imagination. These are the patterns of the abstract and representational arts. These are the shapes of our dreams and our day-time reveries. These are the forms in our fears, our wishes, and our fantasies. It is not surprising, then, that these should also be the mark of our phantasms and telepathic impressions. Regardless of their sources and mechanisms, telepathic impressions have the quality of unconscious symbolism, of the eternal symbols found on all levels of development of man, at all stages of maturation, and in all cultures.

No student of the mind—however mind is conceived and defined—whether he is a psychiatrist, psychologist, philosopher, or artist, can afford to neglect the outstanding and simple truth that images, in waking or sleeping, are often described in the form of symbols that are beyond conscious command. That some of these have no known objective source we already know from psychology. Many of them are related to what are usually called psychical phenomena, which become even more interesting when we recognize that they occur in similar psychological contexts and obey the same laws as other mental manifestations.

In preparing this manuscript for the American reader, it was necessary to elaborate what the author presented with Gallic brevity. The elaborations are largely in the form of descriptions of experiments from other writings of the author and in making more explicit some of the ideas implicit in the original lecture.

Generalizations are illustrated by experiments in which special phenomena are demonstrated. The experiments reported are a small fraction of the total number. The drawings speak for themselves. All references to the literature, primary as well as secondary sources, are incorporated in the running notes at the end of the book. A bibliography is also included, in which the reader will find ready reference for most aspects of the problem he may wish to pursue. There is a glossary of terms, not only those used by the author in a special sense, but also more general concepts from psychology and psychical research. The index will prove helpful to those who will want to find again some of the suggestive ideas with which the book is replete. All works cited will be found in the bibliography.

It would indeed be remiss if gratitude were not expressed to: Mrs. Laura Abbott Dale and Dr. Montague Ullman, for having read the early drafts and for having provided invaluable suggestions; Miss Dorothy A. Buck, for assisting in the preparation of the manuscript; the American Society for Psychical Research, for its interest and cooperation; and Mrs. Eileen J. Garrett, for making the publication of this manuscript possible.

Emanuel K. Schwartz

I INTRODUCTION

PROGRESS in psychical research in recent decades has taken many divergent forms, some of which are almost unknown even to workers in this field. Many today will think only of exact laboratory studies of extrasensory perception, with elaborate controls and statistical treatment; others will think of new studies of apparitions, phantasms, or hauntings; still others will take note of the increasing interest of psychoanalysts in the telepathic factor in dreams and in the unconscious interplay between patients and their analysts.

One may nevertheless feel with justice that the question of the real nature of telepathy is central to almost all of the issues that come up; for telepathy, the oldest of the experimental problems with which psychical research has dealt systematically, is a problem upon which ever more light needs to be thrown. Those acquainted with the field are surely interested no longer in sheer masses of data thrust down their throats in an attempt to make them believe something. On the contrary, interest has turned primarily to the question of dynamics. If telepathy exists, what is its rationale, its meaning? Here a clear hypothesis pursued patiently through years of work is worth far more than some vast, cosmic generalization beyond all experimental test, all verification.

And here, surely, the raw stuff of everyday telepathic impressions, as they occur in dreams or in the waking state, would seem to have for the study of dynamics many advantages over those rigidly defined and controlled events in which one must always choose between one out of five prepared symbols or one out of fifty-two cards in a deck. Problems of experimental and statistical control haunt us, of course, throughout every use of such free material. It is certainly true that in the case of any one specific impression that one mind may seem to catch from another mind we can never honestly close the door upon an interpretation in terms of coincidence; nor can we honestly say even with a handful of such cases that we have proven under what types of conditions telepathy works best. We do, however, come back to one very simple, very fundamental fact: nature throws at us a great deal of material in the form of impressions, usually pictorial, regarding what other people are thinking. And if we will take nature as she is rather than as we think she ought to be, there may be a huge value in steadfastly studying over the years the question of such correspondences between the thoughts of one man and another.

II

NOW this is exactly what René Warcollier and his group of research collaborators have been trying to do since the opening years of this century. The story of this man and his group may be worth telling in some detail as a way of making more personal contact with the research data that are to follow.

Warcollier, a young chemical engineer, established himself before World War I through an invention for the manufacture of artificial jewelry from the scales of fish. Factories were opened in France and in the United States, and he settled down to a relatively steady and safe type of engineering productivity. In collaboration with some friends, shortly before 1910, he began to attempt two types of telepathic experimentation which seemed to be justified by the French psychological work that he had been reading. First, he would attempt to transmit pictures from the mind of an active experimenter or "agent" to the relaxed and passive mind of a subject, or "percipient" who lay in a state of semi-sleep. Second, he would attempt, by a method similar to that of the Polish investigator, Ochorowicz, to influence the normal course of free association, using games of chance in such a way as to allow telepathic impulses to guide the hand of the percipient to one rather than to another card. He had finished in the Spring of 1914 a volume entitled *La Télépathie,* but the sudden outbreak of World War I in July forced him to postpone publication. Clapped into the army straight from his quiet, sedentary life as an engineer, he was packed off under "heavy marching order" some forty kilometers until he was literally so weary as to be "supremely indifferent to the question whether he was to live or to die." Then, as suddenly, he was drawn from the ranks by a telegram and sent into a technical engineering unit for the duration of the war.

In 1919 he resumed his peace-time engineering tasks and ardently began to work again on his studies in telepathy. In 1922 he set up in France and in various other European countries little "telepathic posts," or research centers, which were to communicate telepathically with one another. The usual procedure was to agree through correspondence which group was to act as a "battery of agents" and which group was to act as a "battery of percipients," the formal report of each group crossing the other in the mail. Through communications with Carl Vett, Secretary of the International Congresses of Psychical Research, it was my privilege to get in touch with Warcollier in 1922, and I stopped for a holiday visit with him in Paris in 1923. Here we made arrangements for a series of transatlantic experiments. The results are briefly noted in the work to follow. They were formally reported by Warcollier himself at the Third International Congress of Psychical Research, held in Paris in 1927.

In the period of the 1920s, Warcollier's productivity in the field of telepathy became tremendous. The volume *La Télépathie,* publication of which had been postponed because of the war, appeared in 1921. It soon sold five thousand copies and became a classic to the French reader in the area of parapsychology. There followed in the *Revue Métapsychique* a long series of brilliant analytical studies dealing with the nature of the telepathic processes. What is it that is transmitted? How does it transmit itself? What are the dynamics of the telepathic impulse? What is its relation to time and to space, to imagery, to the dream, and to the whole area of the unconscious? Here, systematically and a step at a time, were presented detailed experimental materials from the weekly sessions both of the Paris group, which he himself conducted, and of the other collaborating groups, including our own New York group.

In 1929 my wife, my mother, and I had the pleasure of a three weeks' visit with Warcollier, his generous and hospitable wife, his eager and friendly *belle-soeur,* and his impish and delightful son, then just beginning to contemplate preparation for a career in medicine. There in Brittany, at the old town of Pont-Aven, we discussed for hours at a time, in the huge orchard, the questions which Janet, Grasset, Myers, and others had raised regarding the subconscious, and the implications of Henri Bergson's philosophy for the problem of transcending time and space. During a part of this visit, S. G. Soal joined us from Great Britain and eagerly participated in the discussion of experimental and quantitative methods in telepathic research.

After 1929 our contacts were continued through a steady flow of correspondence. Interest centered about the question of the nature of the telepathic image, the "fragmentation" of the impulse, the role of emotion and of movement in starting the liberation from the subconscious of those memory traces which are capable of repeating the theme present in the original stimulus. He constantly asked for information about new psychological experiments, such as the exciting studies of eidetic imagery coming from Marburg and from

American laboratories, and he noted with interest new studies in physiological psychology, such as the demonstration of layers in the cerebral cortex related to different aspects of perceived objects, such as color, shape, and size. He was at this time still having weekly lunches with the great physiologist, Charles Richet, and his love of physiology, and of physics and chemistry, was constantly evident in all these new studies and speculations.

Warcollier had been close to Dr. Geley when the latter was director of the *Institut Métapsychique,* and he continued as an associate of Dr. Osty after Dr. Geley's death; in fact, he was charged with telepathy studies and began to play a more and more important role in the editing of the *Revue Métapsychique.*

It had been agreed one day in the orchard at Pont-Aven that an American edition of Warcollier's work would be prepared. The problem proved to be very complex, because it became more and more evident that the best of his research and systematic interpretation lay in the articles in the *Revue Métapsychique* appearing in the twenties and early thirties, rather than in the volume, *La Télépathie,* of 1921. After much reflection, it was decided that only a few chapters from the original book would be translated, but that many of the articles from the *Revue Métapsychique* would be used and integrated with the book material. There was also some material deriving from work carried out in 1935 when, for the moment, he held the title of Research Officer of the Boston Society for Psychic Research, a nominal arrangement made for the purpose of facilitating the continuation of the studies in Paris. The generous services of Mrs. Josephine B. Gridley were obtained for the translation, and the aid of Drs. Ernest Taves and J. G. Pratt proved invaluable in the completion of the task of editing this work, which appeared in 1938 with the imprint of the Boston Society for Psychic Research and in a slightly abbreviated form as a Harper book under the titles, respectively, of *Experimental Telepathy* and *Experiments in Telepathy.*

In 1940 communication with Warcollier ceased suddenly. For four years there could be no parapsychology in France. I shall never forget the dramatic moment in July, 1944, when an American newspaper correspondent at Caen managed to get a cable through to me from Warcollier's son, Dr. Pierre Warcollier, reporting that he and the whole family were well. This was almost in the very hour of the liberation of Caen by American troops, and Pierre and his father had turned to us with the good tidings.

Finally recognition came to Warcollier from the French world of savants; he was asked in June of 1946 to address the Sorbonne. This address was to contain, in one brief sketch, typical examples of the telepathic process and a theory showing the probable relations of telepathy to other processes of communication in which the living organism takes part. This is the substance of the present booklet. It must not, however, be concluded that this is a summary of Warcollier's work, presented in a few pages. For it is very doubtful whether this lifetime of work can be compressed into so short a compass. Actually what is involved is the development of a few simple, cardinal ideas, and enough illustrative material to enable the reader to ruminate on the problem. The very last thing in the world that the author would be interested in insisting upon would be the value of this little book as *proof* of telepathy. We are dealing here with hypotheses about the ultimate nature of telepathy, worn "like loose garments" to see how well they look and at what points they might tear. It is quite likely that time will show that for every good hypothesis there is a bad one. The only trouble is that we cannot be sure at this time which is good and which is bad. We must take them all in an inquiring, detached spirit, and see how far they fit our own experience.

III

WHILE I should not like to oversimplify what is already much simplified in the text which follows, I feel I should attempt my own statement of the primary theoretical considerations which this work seems to present.

First, we have the thought that telepathy is a primitive process, a process less developed, less differentiated than rational thought, a process reminiscent of types of communication between insects or perhaps some of the herd animals.

This primitive, "global," or undifferentiated kind of mental activity belongs less sharply to any one individual as distinct from another than does, say, a rational conviction. Those who are less sharply divided from one another because they are less developed are most capable of telepathic rapport. This may include primitive men, little children, and perhaps persons in various states of enfeeblement or disease. If the reader will take note of another volume appearing at about this time, Dr. Jan Ehrenwald's *Telepathy and Medical Psychology,* he will find developed more fully the notion that telepathic phenomena may spring from a very primitive need to compensate for what is defective or inadequate in the functioning of the living organism, a point which presents several facets reminiscent of the Warcollier thesis.

Second, partly because it is primitive, the telepathic process is not concerned with those sharply defined objects in the world of time and space to which words point and with which scientific thought is usually concerned. As with Bergson, so with Warcollier: the primitive, the impulsive, the crudely dynamic, we might say, that which bespeaks our wishes and our fears, is more likely to reduplicate itself from mind to mind. It may, to be sure, carry along with it—it may, so to speak, "volatilize"—rational material. Those deeply anxious about an air raid, for example, may convey to one another the shape of the dreaded bomber. But it is the emotion and the impulse that provide the dynamic. As far as we know, the raw impulse, as a matter of sheer muscular tension moving toward activity and release, operates here as does emotion. Both *emotion* and *movement* can be set in contrast to the world of orderly thought.

Third, as the telepathic impulse takes shape, it wells up into the consciousness of the receiver or "percipient" and takes the form of images. These images may be distorted as are dream images whose symbolism calls for interpretation. Indeed, they may undergo all the processes which dream images undergo. Along with condensation and simplification, they may show reduplication, so that a curve or an angle tells the story, so to speak, over and over again. A primitive process of classification is also evident, in which there is a sort of alignment or grouping of materials which are similar. As a result of all these distorting processes, the end result may lose the original meaning and yet prove to be reducible to the same sensory elements, the same lines and colors, with which one began. Here, of course, one needs a great deal of convergent evidence from different subjects, and, it should be added, a type of experimental control which has proved to be as difficult to develop in free telepathic material as in the free materials developed by psychoanalytic studies. There is, however, a certain internal corroboration, a certain regularity and consistency, a certain lawfulness, which appear also in apparitions and other types of spontaneous telepathy.

The question arises whether, by noting all these general principles, one can learn to prepare oneself for telepathic reception. Can one train oneself in the detection of genuine telepathic impulses, sifting them out, cultivating them, and at the same time learning to discard or put into a separate category those images which are purely subjective in origin? Warcollier's own personal experience, from which illustrations are drawn over a period of several decades, is one of the interesting lines of evidence that such training in telepathic reception is possible. The reader who is deeply interested will test for himself whether or not training in the telepathic process is possible.

IV

WE HAVE been describing an address given at the Sorbonne, and summing up a few of its ideas. After Mrs. E. de P. Matthews had worked through this material first, and Mrs. J. B. Gridley had made a more formal attempt, in keeping with her earlier task of translating the Warcollier volume so as to render these ideas in brief and readable English, the decision was reached, in consultation with the publisher, to attempt a much more radical alteration of the text in a form more suitable for the American public. To Dr. Emanuel K. Schwartz fell the task not of translating but of completely reorganizing this over-condensed French presentation for the general American reader interested in telepathic research. I wish to add my own tribute to Dr. Schwartz's work; for only a very energetic and a very devoted prosecution of this task could prove adequate to the problem of rendering for the American reader the subtle and complex observations which Warcollier had made. While repeating the fact that it would be impossible to summarize Warcollier's lifetime of telepathic research in so brief a compass, I would stress that Dr. Schwartz has brought out as clearly and forcibly as is humanly possible the relation between the Sorbonne address and the earlier work of Warcollier, as exemplified in *La Télépathie* and in his articles in the *Revue Métapsychique.*

V

A WORD about the way in which this study "fits into" the framework of psychical research as it exists today. With the successful inauguration of large-scale university research in parapsychology by Dr. J. B. Rhine, there is no danger that the academic world will lapse back into the supreme indifference to these problems which had previously characterized it. The work of Rhine consists very largely of ascertaining the amount of extrasensory perception which may occur under certain rigidly defined experimental conditions, and in which we note refined statistical techniques used in demonstrating that the results are not attributable to chance artifacts. There is no doubt whatever that this vast experimental program, involving literally millions of individual attempts to make contact with hidden or distant target materials, constitutes the corner-stone of modern experimental parapsychology. At the same time, we find Rhine and his associates, J. G. Pratt, B. Humphrey, and, above all, the late C. E. Stuart, concerning themselves with the use of free drawings—both with the problem of the statistical evaluation of results which seem to transcend chance expectation and with the dynamics of the telepathic communication of such drawings.

The extensive studies of the transmission of free drawings by the late Whately Carington in England may, moreover be regarded as a bridge between the Warcollier approach and the Rhine approach, in the sense that Carington's method was consistently to use pictorial material drawn from a very extensive collection, rather than to pin the subject down to a choice between a few possibilities. Carington was unremitting in his efforts to develop a sound statistical procedure for the evaluation of the results of this method. One might, then, if one liked the figure of speech, think of Warcollier as standing on one bank of the river where one defines qualitatively the nature of the materials which may at times appear in telepathic communication. On the other bank stand those who are ready to define sharply and to measure quantitatively all that appears in a carefully prepared telepathic experiment. The bridge from one bank to the other consists of the Carington type of statistics for the study and evaluation of pictorial material. This analogy is, of course, inadequate in many ways, for it leaves out Rhine's concern with unconscious dynamics and Carington's concern with the laws of association which, he believed, operate in telepathic communication. Most serious, from the point of view developed here, is the fact that the analogy leaves out of account the rich philosophical background and the subtle use of the material from psychopathology and the psychology of primitives and children that appear in Warcollier's work. The image of the bridge will, however, have to serve in a rough way.

The author himself would be the first to insist that this little booklet should be seen in perspective as but one part of a vast enterprise and not as the final word. If it leads the reader to become intrigued with the psychological questions that it raises, and if it tempts him to learn how to cross the bridge from daily experience to the world of exact experimental control and exact statistical evaluation, so that each day of his life he is ready and able to move easily back and forth from one to the other, integrating the two, then it will abundantly have served its purpose.

Gardner Murphy

I FRAME OF REFERENCE

MANY OF YOU have had personal experiences that seem to suggest telepathy. You may have shared by word of mouth the inexplicable events in the lives of others that have for centuries made up the lore of psychical phenomena. In the last one hundred years these spontaneous occurrences have been systematically recorded and investigated.[1] Groups of reputable workers throughout the world have been turning their attention not only to the manifestations of telepathy in real-life situations, but also to the careful study of the telepathic process under experimental conditions. I shall use the word "telepathy" as did Frederic W. H. Myers, who coined it in 1882. Telepathy includes the communication of emotions, ideas, mental images, sensations, or words from one individual to another without the help of the senses.

At colleges and universities experiments in telepathy are being conducted, and a mass of data has accumulated. Many outstanding men of science, especially British and American, have been concerned with the problem of telepathy in order to establish, without question, its existence. The conditions under which it arises spontaneously and experimentally, and the psychological and physiological mechanisms involved, are being studied. Telepathy has not yet been accepted by science in general. On the other hand, institutions of higher learning have been recognizing the academic contributions of parapsychologists, as in the case of the Cambridge mathematician, S. G. Soal, who has recently been awarded the degree of Doctor of Science by the University of London for the experimental work in telepathy he did during World War II. Moreover, psychiatrists, psychoanalysts, and psychologists have become increasingly aware of the need for understanding telepathy as a human experience.

Nearly forty years ago a series of telepathic dreams awakened my interest in this field.[2] Since then I have devoted myself to a study of the problems of telepathy. It does not seem that my time and effort have been wasted. Observation has confirmed my earlier feelings that telepathic communication does exist. Fraudulent cases exist, but they are not the whole story. Nor do I believe that a theory of chance coincidence can explain more than a few of the facts.

Some of my friends also became interested, and we decided to conduct a series of experiments in telepathy. In most of our experiments we used drawings, as did other investigators, because they allow more precise check and control than do thoughts and verbal ideas.[3] We were not professional subjects; we used no elaborate techniques or complicated devices. All of the experiments were conducted in the waking state. One of us would serve as sender or agent and another as receiver or percipient. Generally, a time would be set when the agent was to concentrate on an image spontaneously selected by him, which he then drew immediately. Simultaneously the percipient focused his attention on the agent, cleared his mind of all thoughts, and noted the mental images appearing in his consciousness. These impressions he, too, drew at once. Each participant sent his drawings and comments to the other members of the team. Letters crossed in the mail and postmarks showed the time and place of the experiment. Occasionally, we varied the method, as you will soon see, in accordance with special objectives and circumstances.

It was under these conditions of good faith, and with a sense of serious responsibility and cooperation, that a series of experiments unfolded over the years. We sought telepathically to transmit drawings from one room to another, from one quarter of Paris to another, from one city to another, and from one country to another. Distance never seemed to affect the results.[4] The findings were not always positive. As a matter of fact, over the entire period of forty years, comparatively few of our experiments were successful if the results are interpreted very strictly. Only a fraction of the telepathic impressions were indisputable hits when compared with the targets. On the other hand, for ten years a group of a dozen friends worked together once a week at the *Institut Métapsychique International* in Paris and achieved meaningful results in more than half of the cases. In every experiment I participated either as agent or percipient.

The material I am presenting here does not deal primarily with the success or the lack of success in the telepathic transmission of drawings. Nor do I wish to demonstrate the existence of telepathy, for the British and American research workers have been applying themselves to this problem with statistical methods. Their quantitative results afford strong evidence for telepathy. My purpose is to share observations of what actually happens in the telepathic communication of drawings. Certain dynamic principles suggest themselves which are similar to those found in psychology. In our investigations we have noted that the laws of normal and abnormal perception seem to apply to telepathy. Paranormal mental imagery reveals characteristics like those found in normal forms of experience, such as dreams and eidetic imagery.[5] I have devoted the body of this book to a presentation of these dynamic laws and illustrative cases.

One evening I was visiting my friends, Mr. and Mrs. Archat. After dinner we attempted the telepathic transmission of a drawing. Mr. Archat, an electrical engineer, acted as agent. I was the percipient, and Mrs. Archat the note-taker. Mr. Archat remained in the dining room behind closed doors. Mrs. Archat and I went to rooms at the other end of the floor. Mrs. Archat recorded my impressions as I dictated them. The target was a dirigible (Fig. 1).[6] I sensed that my first impression, a bread basket with a roll-down top, was wrong. If my efforts had ended at this point, the trial might have been judged a failure. In reality, however, this first image was made up of a synthesis of the idea of rotation and of an impression of the mass of the balloon. It took the form of a bread basket associated with the idea of a connecting rod and shaft which I drew. My second impression was correct, namely, a profile view of a screw propeller shaped like the number 8. Then, by introspection, I recognized the inaccuracy of the roll-down-top image. Immediately after remarking that I was in good form, I perceived the outline of the dirigible and began to draw it, using the earlier partial impressions. The drawings were made before I recognized the dirigible. No conscious association of ideas of that day or of preceding days could be revived by any of us to label this a coincidence. It is my feeling that the perception of the target may be explained only by means of the latent idea of rotation. The impression of movement is quite typical of this entire class of telepathic experiences.

The telepathic image is not transmitted in the same way as a wireless photo. The image is scrambled, broken up into component elements which are often transmuted into a new pattern. It seldom arrives complete and organized. A telepathic image resembles somewhat a chemical molecule. The original molecule, the target, decomposes into elements. Some of these elements are received and are recombined into a new molecular structure. There are emotional and intellectual elements in the psychic molecule which always strives to maintain a stable internal organization. The emotional or affective components are of great importance and form the basis of spontaneous telepathy. Emotional states tend to be more easily perceived than intellectual material. It is extremely difficult

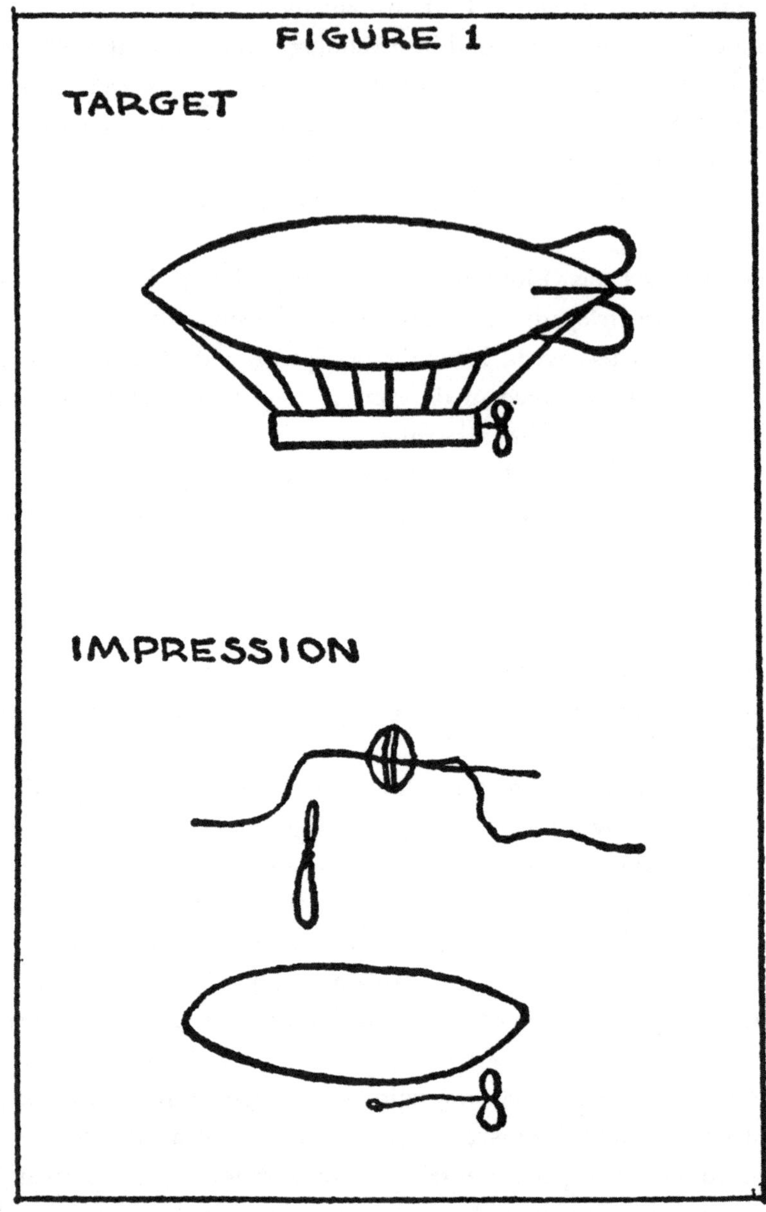

telepathically to communicate purely intellectual images, such as letters of the alphabet. On the other hand, it must not be forgotten that Rhine and his collaborators have done much fundamental experimental work, using the ESP cards almost exclusively. Each of the ESP cards bears one of five abstract intellectual symbols; namely, star, square, circle, waves (three parallel wavy lines), and plus.

I PARALLELISM

IN THIS CONNECTION we wanted to find out what would happen with simple geometric figures. They represent a form of abstract intellectual image. We conducted a series of studies and discovered that they behave peculiarly in telepathic communication. A square is received not as four straight lines, but as two or more right angles scattered in space (Fig. 2). This is a good example of successful telepathic transmission, even though the impression is not identical with the original drawing. The rectangle enclosing five egg-shaped figures was received as five egg-shaped figures and four right angles scattered in space. The dispersion of elements occurs also with other geometric figures. Concentric circles are often received as nests of detached arcs and as detached circles (Fig. 3). Other investigators had similar findings; e.g., Sinclair (Fig. 4), (Fig. 5) and (Fig. 6), and Usher and Burt (Fig. 7).[1]

What seems to happen in the case of geometric figures is that movement is injected into what would otherwise be a static image. Movement is a dynamic of "unclosed" or open configurations and usually implies activity. The squares and circles are static figures; the angles and arcs scattered in space are open or dynamic. It is almost as if we had for telepathy no memory trace of specific geometric figures, such as the rectangle and the circle. Instead we possess only angles and arcs. These elements align themselves in a variety of positions and tend to match themselves one to another. There is a sort of mutual attraction between suitable parts, a kind of grouping which I should like to call "the law of parallelism," that like seeks like. In my opinion, it is entirely a question of patterns of movement; that is, parallelism is a way for the image to achieve a simple organization. The simpler the diagram and the less experienced the subject, the easier it is to detect this process. In metagnomes, that is, special sensitives who may have the capacity to describe experiences and even whole

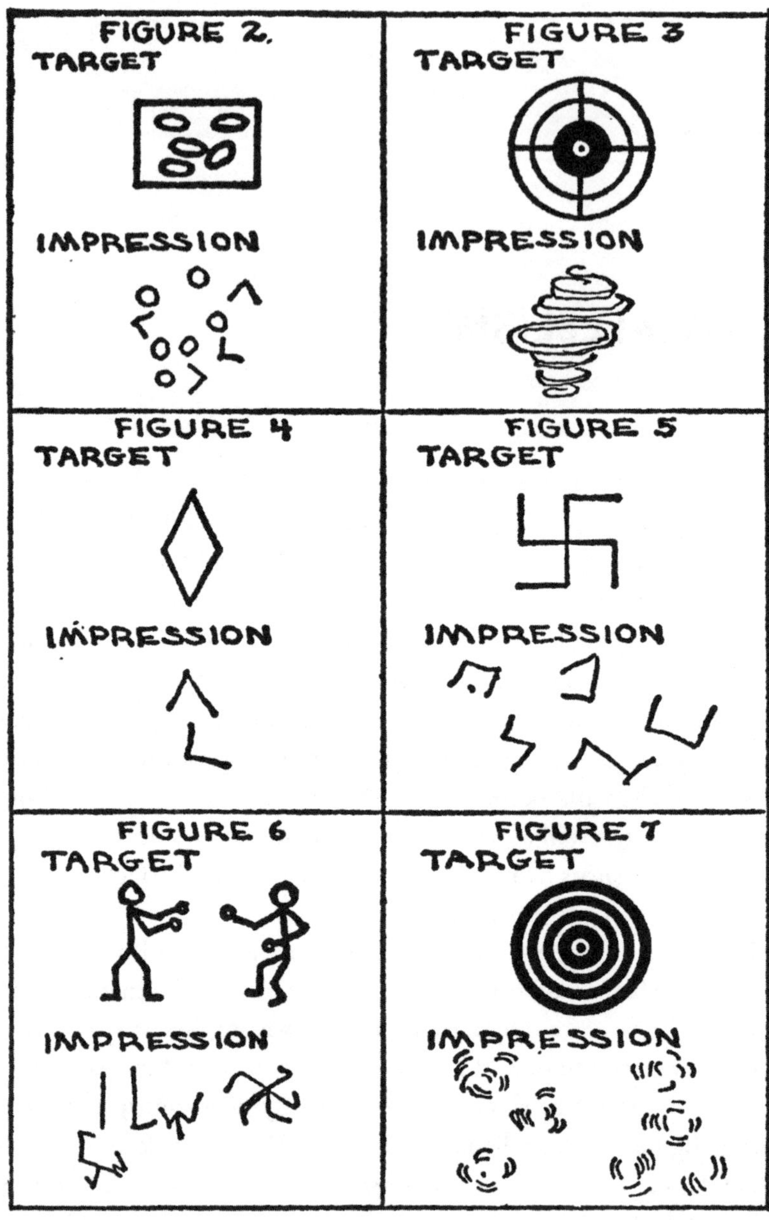

scenes out of the life of a person, the laws of telepathy seem to be obscured. We shall have to concern ourselves, nevertheless, with describing those processes which seem to be essential and operative in all telepathic communication whether they are obvious or not.

I LATENCY

PARANORMAL EVENTS BRING sharply into focus not only our concept of space, but of time, as well.[1] Paranormal perception does not seem to be dependent upon or limited by time. As we shall presently see, timing is a highly individual matter. Experiments in precognition or non-inferential foreknowledge, that is, the direct perception of future events, suggest that there is a constant and optimal tempo for each percipient. Timing seems to be related to individual rhythms, incentives and needs, stemming from the depths of the personality.

Our experience points to the fact that telepathic communication is not instantaneous. The telepathic image is not received at the same moment it is sent. There is a certain lag in time which I refer to as the phenomenon of latency. This delay, as in our experiments with drawings, can last a few seconds or a few minutes, or it may extend over several days. If I may be permitted another analogy from the physical sciences, we have here something that resembles an exposed but undeveloped photographic negative. This is the latent image. An unconscious model or psychic context from which the figure gradually evolves can be seen also in the distortions of children's drawings and in eidetic imagery. It may be during this period of latency that the elements become distorted or that they reconstitute themselves into new patterns. Moreover, secondary elaboration takes place which frequently gives rise to a large number of associations that attach themselves to the impression that is received when a drawing is the telepathic target.

The Polish engineer, Ossowiecki, was an unusually sensitive subject. He was once asked to perceive a concealed drawing consisting of a circle, a triangle, and a square laid out on a single sheet of paper (Fig. 8). He began by describing "a circle" and "probably a triangle." He did not see the third figure clearly. He drew a circle and then a triangle, but lowered its base and converted it into

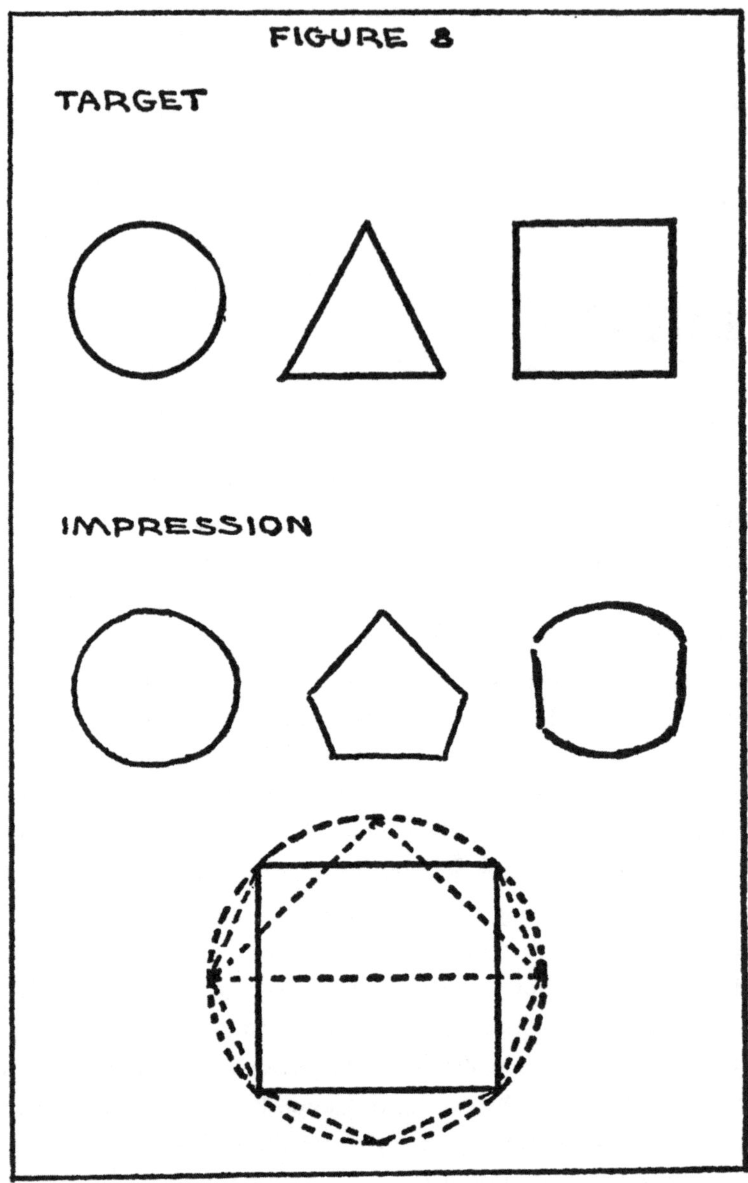

a polygon. Instead of the square he started to draw a circle and converted it finally into an octagon. Obviously there was a reciprocal influencing of the various figures. The circle affected the square to the point of inhibiting it almost completely; and the square altered the triangle. It seemed almost as if the three figures were superimposed, one upon the other, in the unconscious of the receiver (see my dotted line drawing). In this way, a kind of latent negative was formed from which three different and distinct positives were drawn successively. Since the unconscious negative was a composite, it is only natural that the effect of any one figure should be felt in the others. On the other hand, Ossowiecki placed each figure on the page in the same position as in the target. By this he demonstrated the existence also of a global impression of the spatial arrangement. He must have had an idea of three figures placed in a certain relationship on the page; otherwise he might have drawn a kind of contaminated single figure, as I have tried to indicate.

Immediately after the preceding experiment, Ossowiecki did a life reading of the experimenter. In commenting upon the background as perceived by Ossowiecki, Professor Barrington-Emerson said, "You have described the contents of several rooms, but the locations of the furniture were confused. . . . On the whole, your descriptions here are as exact and precise as in the case of the geometric figures, despite the fact that some of the details are a little vague. It is evident that you were capable of reading my thoughts with exactitude and clarity."[2]

Another celebrated sensitive, Pascal Forthuny, once described a particular quarter of a city known to the experimenter, Dr. François Moutier. Moutier commented, "All that Mr. Forthuny has just said is accurate. But it is really as if someone had taken the elements of a scene and had heaped them one upon another in arrangement and perspective differing slightly from reality."[3]

In these experiments the same process recurs. I should like to offer the hypothesis that a latent image is formed. In the process of its formation the elements begin to reveal themselves to the conscious mind. This takes place as a series of discharges like the progressive appearance of details on a photographic negative in a developing solution.

I DISSOCIATION

ONE ASPECT OF our general theory is the irrational and mechanistic decomposition of the target into elements. This analytic process I call "dissociation." Not all percipients decompose or dissociate a telepathic impression to the same extent. Imperfections in the telepathic image arise more often in the receiving than in the sending. Reception is due to successive discharges of the components of the telepathic model or latent image from the percipient's unconscious into his conscious. These discharges do not resemble vague thoughts or after-images, but disguised symbolic forms that express themselves in a kind of sign or gesture language employing symbols rather than manifest thought-content. An example of the symbolic language of telepathic communication may be seen in the experiment with the eyeglasses (Fig. 9), which I have described in detail in "Le Dessin Télépathique." That target was a drawing of a pair of eyeglasses. The image was received quite clearly and the percipient was able to draw an outline of the form and to describe it in detail. Yet he could not recognize what it was. Sinclair provides a similar example in which the impression is a very accurate outline of the image with the added process of condensation (Fig. 10).[1]

It may be that in the awakening of human consciousness, modes of perception existed which are called into play again in paranormal processes. These sensitivities may provide the basis for such normal psychological phenomena as eidetic imagery. In other types of psychological behavior and in the psychopathology of everyday life the process is similar.[2] A word on the tip of the tongue, for example, is like the telepathic image, in that successive signals arise from the latent model in the unconscious. This is what actually happens in telepathy. We are dealing here, it would seem, with mental powers that suggest an earlier stage of human development.

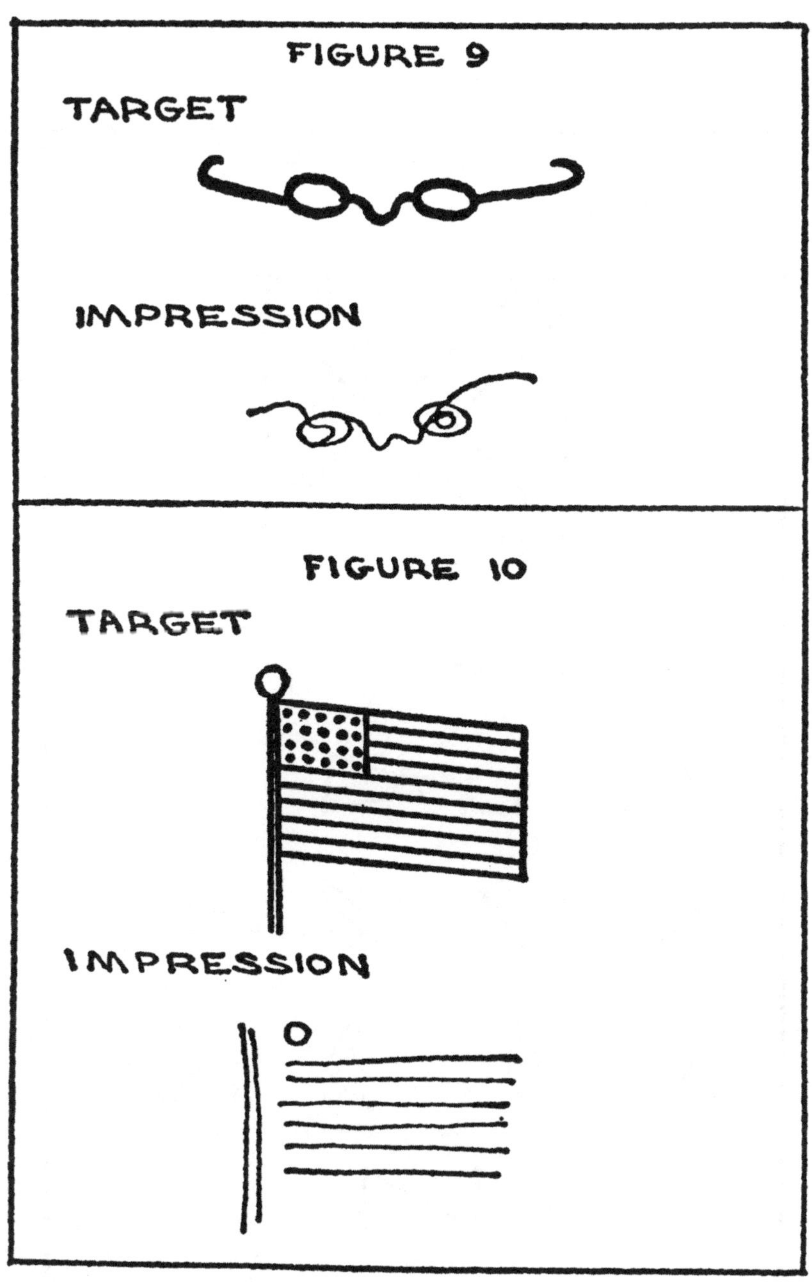

In the experiment with the St. Andrew's Cross, we get a good indication of the process of dissociation in the breakdown of the target (Fig. 11). This dissociation illustrates the process of reception, namely, by means of successive discharges of strong signals.

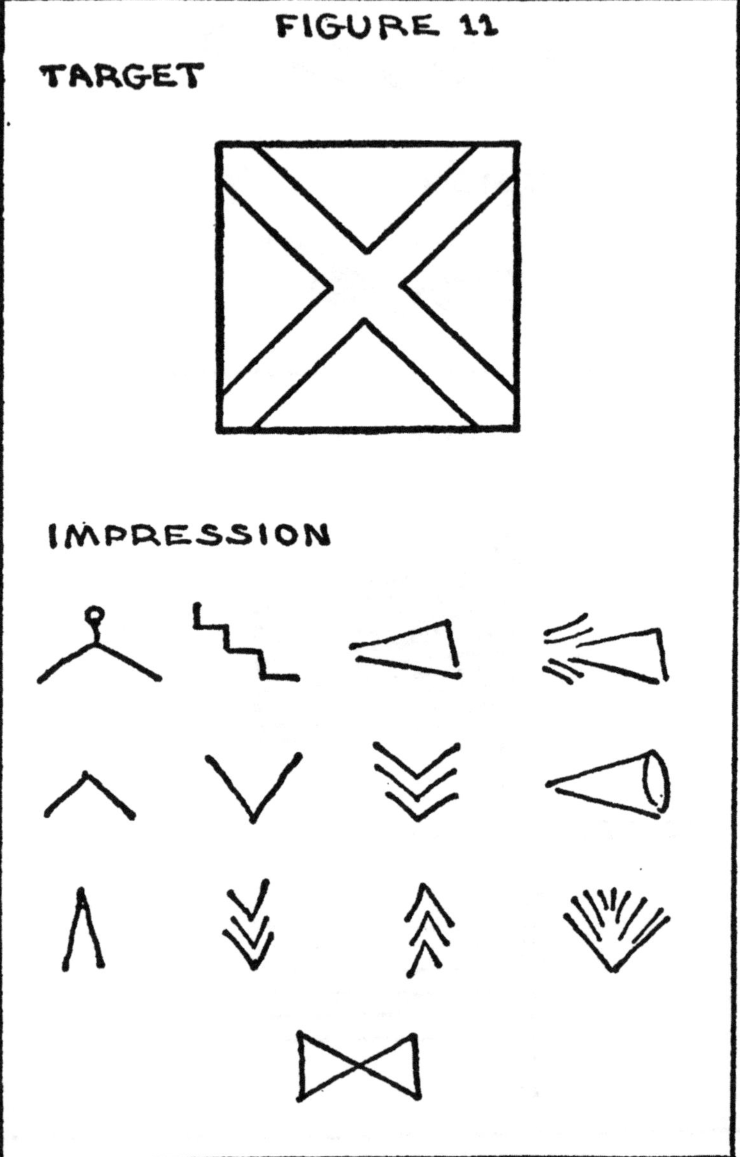
FIGURE 11
TARGET
IMPRESSION

I ANALYSIS

ANALYSIS IS A kind of explosive disintegration of the parts of the image into space. Emotional factors in the receiver may bring about this disintegration. Examples from Sinclair's *Mental Radio* (Fig. 12)[1] and my *Experimental Telepathy* (Fig. 13)[2] illustrate this forcible dispersion. In some cases, the images or parts of the image may be received inverted. In others, the idea of rotation is introduced and it colors the reception.

An agent undertook to send a drawing of Saturn and its rings (Fig. 14). As it was received, the percipient drew the fragmented lines of the top and bottom of the figure. His drawing depicted the rings as they appear at the sides of the target. At the same time, he grasped logically the idea of rotation and expressed it symbolically in the form of a transmission shaft, at the right of his drawing.

Inversion is clearly demonstrated in the experiment with the drops of ink (Fig. 15). Not unlike a photograph where the positive becomes negative, the black spots in the target were reproduced as white spots against a dark background. This is a good example of reversal of figure and ground, and transmission by contrast. The subject in this case said that he saw "a cascade of luminous white balls that were falling." It would seem that the paranormal perception occurred while the drops of ink fell on the paper. The word, "eskri," which the subject said he heard, may be related of the Old French verb, "to write," and can be an association with the idea of pen and ink.

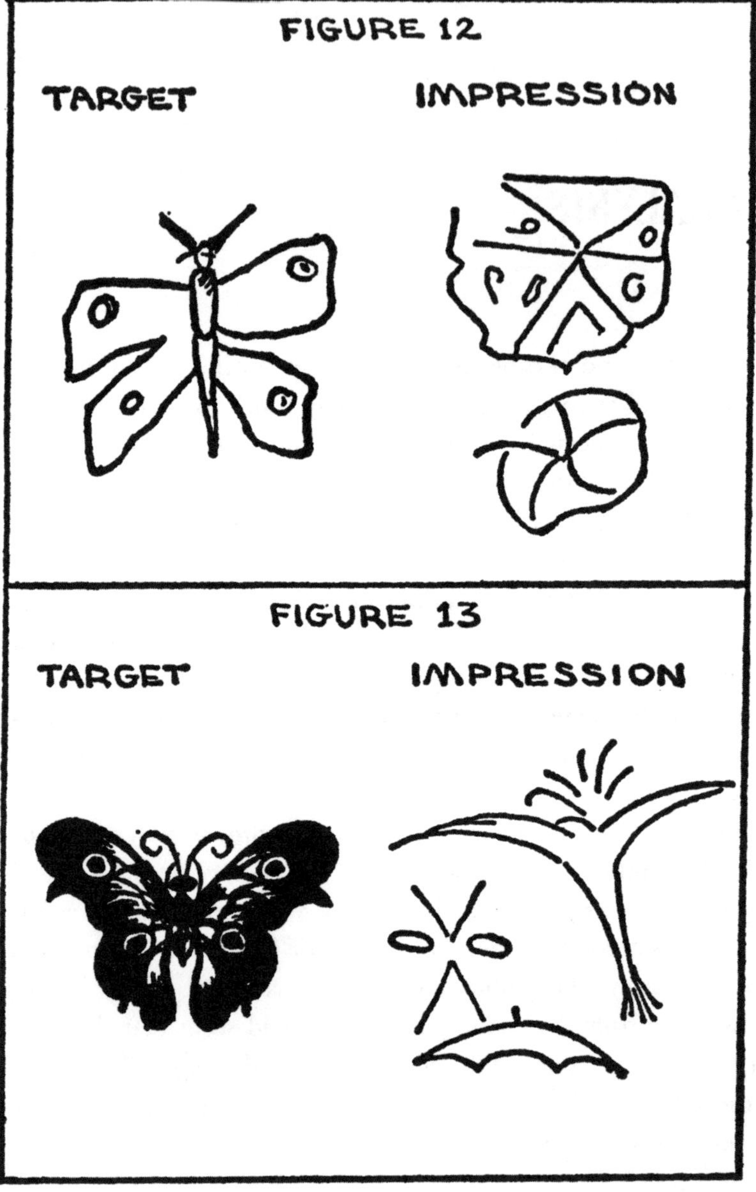
FIGURE 12
TARGET
IMPRESSION
FIGURE 13
TARGET
IMPRESSION

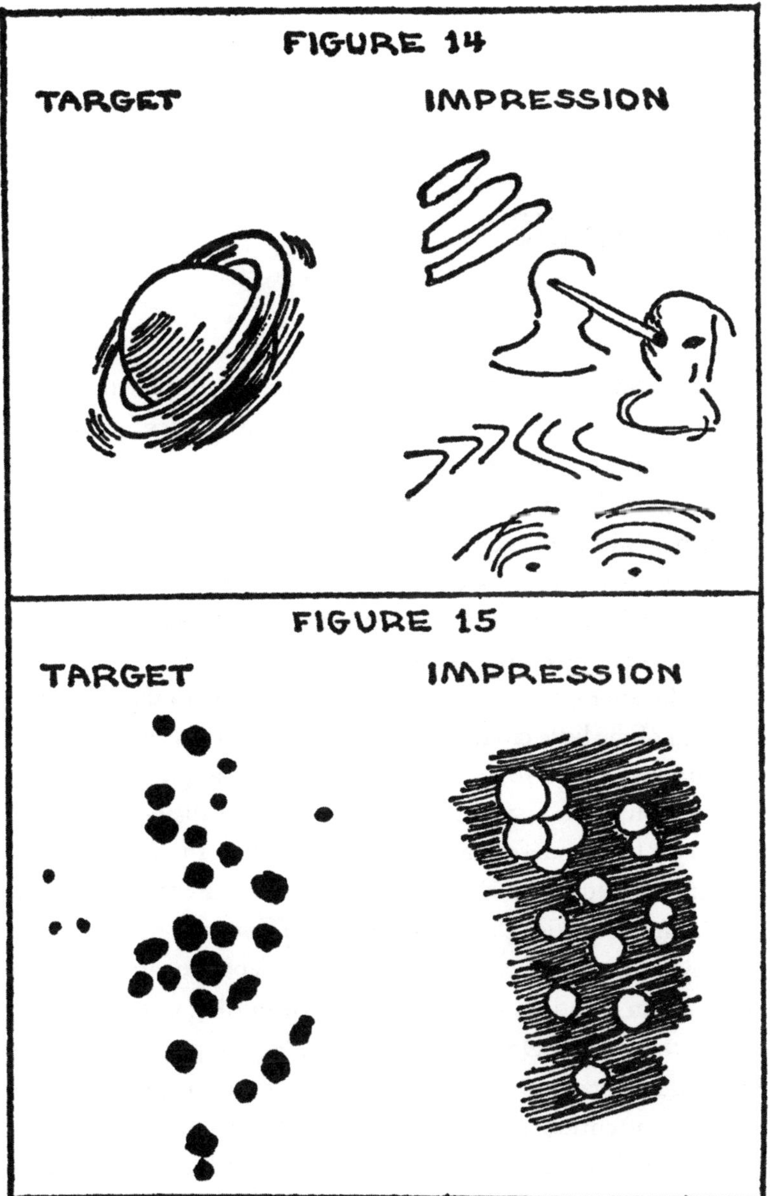
FIGURE 14
TARGET
IMPRESSION
FIGURE 15
TARGET
IMPRESSION

I SYNTHESIS

THE DISSOCIATED ELEMENTS may occasionally duplicate themselves or become reorganized into a meaningful whole. This process, which I call "synthesis," often combines discrete elements withdrawn from the original design and not recognized as parts of it by the receiver. The experiment in which an eye in a triangle was used as a target shows this combinatory process very clearly (Fig. 16). First there was a condensation of the eye and triangle into a double-lined triangular figure, and then a simultaneous multiplication of the shape of the pupil of the eye in a series of successive discharges as smaller circles around the figure. The attempt to synthesize or to apply logic to the elements led only to a grouping of the little circles around the triangle. Here we have logical analysis and synthesis, but no recognition of the original impression.

The question arises as to whether the process of dissociation of the latent impression as I have described it is spontaneous. In cases of spontaneous telepathy the telepathic signal forces itself upon the attention of the percipient. Conversely, under artificial experimental conditions the percipient focuses his attention by means of introspection upon the telepathic target and reaches out for the signal. In addition, there is a continual shifting of the attention to and away from the target. On the one hand, the percipient directs his mental energy toward the target which he disassembles into its psychic elements. On the other, his attention is being constantly distracted by normal sensations from the external environment. The backward and forward movement of the attention in relation to the target determines the staccato character of telepathic reception. The value of hypnosis, drugs and drowsiness for concentration of the attention in a relaxed and receptive state may now be better understood.[1]

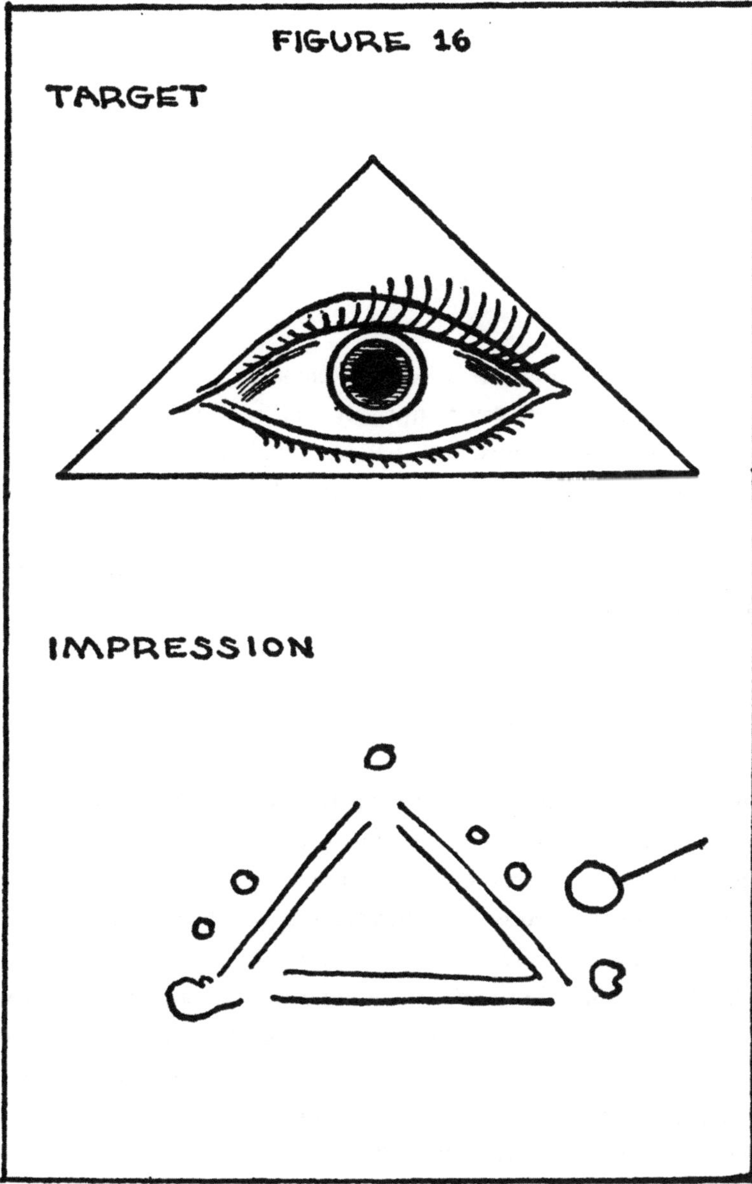
FIGURE 16
TARGET
IMPRESSION

I SYNCRETISM

THERE ARE TIMES, however, when the telepathic impression is received not in piecemeal fashion, but very primitively, that is, globally. What is perceived is the pattern of relationships, and the individual parts remain undefined and jumbled. The perception of the configurational character or wholeness quality of the image without the details, I call "syncretism."

At this point it is not possible to be dogmatic about the method by which the telepathic communication of drawings proceeds. It is likely, however, that telepathic perception always includes both a global impression of the whole as well as a differentiated impression of various parts. In some cases, impression of the parts predominates over the global impression, and the spatial relationships assume less significance. At other times, the components become vague and unimportant and only organization is perceived. I believe that the more primitive and direct intuitive perception is the telepathic reception of a total and undifferentiated impression of the target. An example in which only the global form was perceived is the experiment in which the target was the drawing of a camel and the percipient saw a Capuchin monk (Fig. 17).

It should be pointed out that there appears to be an analogy between the paranormal perception of drawings and the normal perception of drawings exposed for very short periods of time by means of a tachistoscope. As Dworetzki says, "When an impression is obtained very quickly, we grasp the qualities and character of the object by means of syncretic perception. When the lighting is poor or the exposure time particularly short, forms are modified so that only the general outline is seen. Two spots tend to run together and to be fused into a single one; irregularities are overlooked or minimized."[1] Occasionally, however, when a form is perceived syncretically, a particular detail may dominate the impression as in the case of the dirigible (Fig. 1).

In 1930 an attempt was made to demonstrate telepathy at the National Aviation Convention at Vincennes. In casting about for a target, unfortunately the agent selected spontaneously the colored cover of the program. I am including the experiment, nevertheless, because it illustrates fairly consistently some of the processes under discussion. I was to act as the percipient. I received the impression of "cubistic designs in color." The two partial impressions on the left of the drawings (Fig. 18) depict the process of condensation. In telepathy, condensation is essentially the opposite of the process of multiplication and is similar to the condensation typical of dreams. Here it was the reduction

and fusion into a few simple forms the shapes repeated in the target. Note also the appearance again of the idea of movement as a wheel and axle on the right of the drawing. This is another good example of syncretic perception.

I MOVEMENT

IN THE TELEPATHIC transmission of drawings a new factor tends to be introduced very often. Somehow the intellectual components in the latent image become associated with and tied together by some kind of movement. The examples of rotation already reported fit into this category. It was Janet who believed that every idea of an object contains the germ of an act appropriate to it. Movement appears repeatedly in most of our experiments in the telepathic transmission of drawings. The movement factor usually takes dominance over other aspects of what is perceived. In the case of the fan which I discussed in *Experimental Telepathy,* what struck me first was an awareness of opening and closing. This brought to mind the idea of an elbow, and then other elements of the target began to appear (Fig. 19).[1]

The importance of movement in general psychology has already been noted. Children in particular associate movement with concrete objects in the world around them. Much of their language in the beginning is made up of words descriptive of movement. The paranormal perception of drawings resembles this aspect of normal perception. The percipient in telepathy is like the child. When the latent image confronts him, the first thing he observes is movement.

The global and dynamic character of the perception of the child has been investigated by psychologists in many lands. The child does not perceive distinct objects. He sees an "ensemble of movements" associated with the object. He participates, probably unconsciously, in these movements. When he perceives, he really wishes to act, to join in some movement around him. Action precedes visual perception. It is as if the child played with his toys before seeing them. If he recognizes them, it is not because he recognizes the objects in and of themselves, but because he experiences again the repeated movements

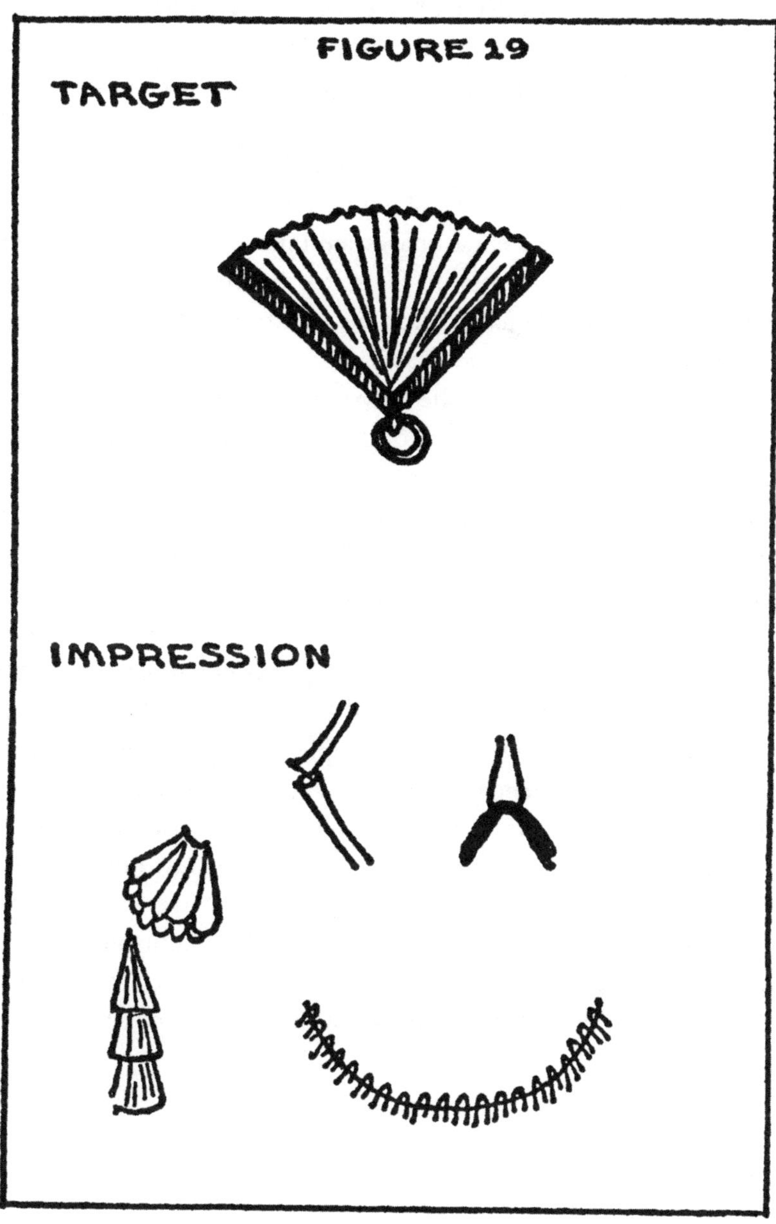

he associates with these objects. A box, even if it cannot be opened, suggests the action of opening. It is the objectified possibility of performing an act; in the case of the box, it consists of raising the lid.

Cousinet writes: "When a child holds out his arms toward a balloon with which a little girl is playing, it is not the balloon that he desires. He scarcely sees the balloon except as a detail of an ensemble. What he wants is the whole ensemble formed by the balloon, the little girl, her gestures and himself. To perceive is for him the wish to act, to make himself part of a more or less complex activity in which the balloon is only a 'pretext.' When one brings him the balloon, he does not recognize the ensemble that he had formerly perceived. One brings him exactly what he had not perceived."[2]

Piéron insists that all mental images are inner gestures. Lipps proposes a "mechanical theory of perception."[3] He states that for every visual act there is the translation of a spatial quality into a motor attitude of our own body. These same attitudes are projected into the image.

It is possible that success in the telepathic communication of drawings is partially dependent upon the ability of the stimulus or target to suggest movement. This may be of some importance for the selection of targets. Moving objects such as a wheel, a propeller, a jack-in-the-box may be good targets because they make the movement "visible" to the agent or sender. I emphasize here those targets in which movement is manifest rather than implied. The jack-in-the-box serves as a good example of how the various types of movement were received (Fig. 20). A spinning top was not perceived as spinning; whereas a man swinging on a horizontal bar was received, even though the impression was well described by the percipient, as a revolving ventilator. An inventory of the simple elements and the component factors in drawings used as targets in telepathic communication would include points, lines, angular and round figures, and random shapes. To these we must now add all of the types of moving things that turn, that go up or down, and that move forward and backward. Variation in size of the targets has little influence upon success in the telepathic communication of drawings. Pratt and Woodruff in their experiments with ESP cards found no significant change in scores with change in symbol size.

FIGURE 20
TARGET
IMPRESSION

I PRÄGNANZ

WE CAN LOOK to the psychology of perception for other principles that reveal themselves in paranormal behavior. The idea of movement in the telepathic impression involves the Gestalt theoretical principle of Prägnanz or precision.[1] The Gestalt theory is advanced by a school of psychology which seeks to understand the wholeness quality or structure of each perception or reaction. The principle of Prägnanz implies that all psychological organization, including perception, strives to be *as good or complete as it can be* under any given set of circumstances. In telepathy we must consider not only the form of movement, but also the quanta or units of movement. It is from this aspect that we may approach some of the more successful of our telepathic experiments.

The principle of Prägnanz brings with it certain other Gestalt theoretical considerations. The relationship between figure and ground in telepathic targets is of significance. The background against which a stimulus appears is for the percipient an important part of the total impression. In one of our experiments we used as a target a jewelry advertisement showing the sparkle of a gem by means of strongly contrasting black and white rays. There were two percipients; I was the agent. The first percipient got the impression of "an acute angle like the letter 'V'; rays; a lighthouse, illuminated," which he then drew. The second percipient noted, "the sensation of repose—a head on a pillow; a vortex of wind; contrast, dark and light; night—a number of small lighted windows." She made a drawing to represent the tornado and a row of small squares for the windows (Fig. 21). The sharp contrast of figure and ground, in this case equally divided and repeated, seems favorable for telepathic communication.

At times there is a parallelism of parts of the stimulus, that is, they seem to group themselves logically (Fig. 22). Sometimes there is repetition of the stimulus or its parts, as described earlier. What we may conclude from our knowl-

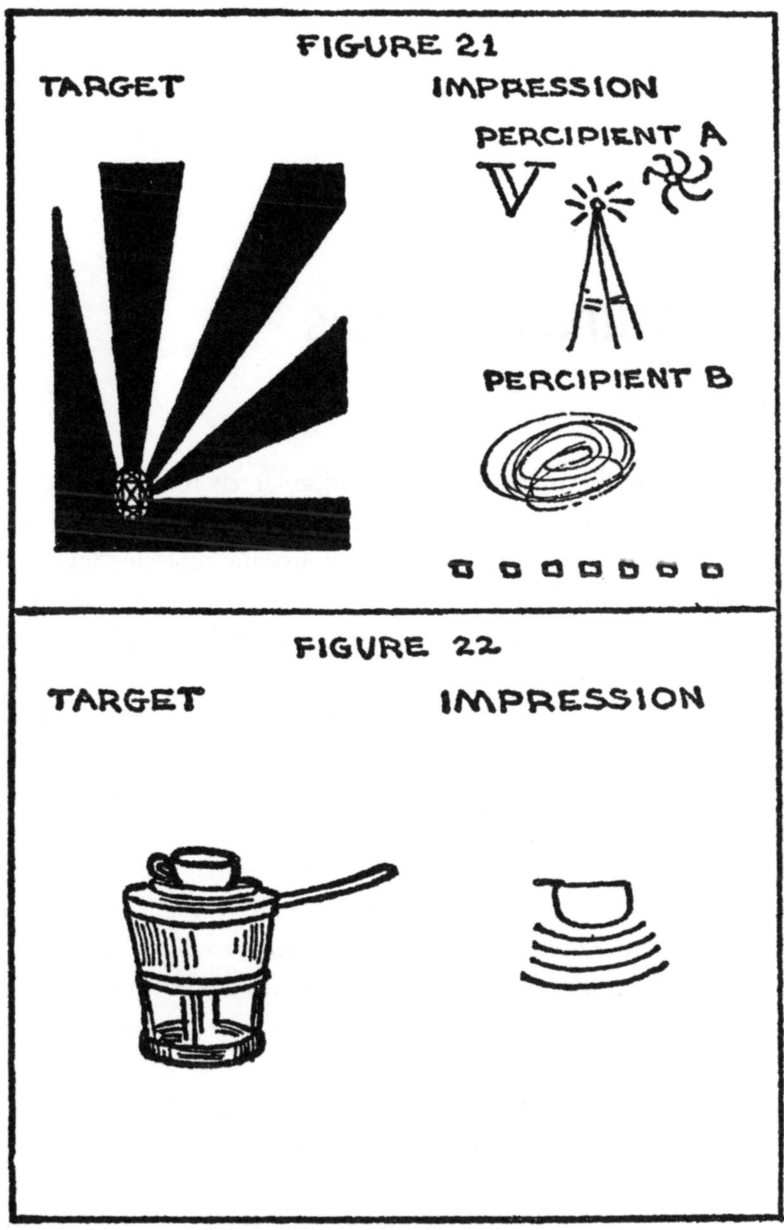

edge of the normal psychology of perception is that there is always a dynamic core in telepathic perception, not unlike that in normal perception, whether the impression is global or detailed. There is a tendency toward organization, toward a wholeness character of the impression, in order that the perception be as simple, as symmetrical, as regular and as meaningful as possible.

I EMOTIONAL FACTORS

UNTIL NOW WE have devoted our attention largely to the intellectual characteristics of the psychic molecule. An attempt has been made to point out how the formal and dynamic aspects of the psychic molecule follow, in telepathic perception, psychological principles derived from normal perception. The psychic molecule, however, is made up of more than one kind of element. In normal as well as paranormal communication, emotional components are extremely important. In certain subjects the emotional factor is dominant. This is true also for some targets which stimulate an emotional reaction in the percipient. They arouse associations which are emotionally significant to him alone. These differences in telepathic reception are most clearly brought out when several percipients participate in the same experiment. Each of the participants seeks in the telepathic target those intellectual and emotional factors which are most meaningful to him and which seem to direct themselves reciprocally to his particular emotional and intellectual constitution. In spontaneous cases of telepathy the individual needs and personality structure seem to be most important.[1]

In normal psychology it has long been known that perception is not purely intellectual and that the total personality, including its emotional components, enters as a whole in the response to a stimulus. Perception always carries with it a varying degree of emotion. Paul Valéry, the French poet, says that this is so because "perception implies an anticipation of the future," that is, a hope or fear in relation to things to come. The telepathic percipient is not an automaton. His consciousness, in response to the latent image, does not operate like a telephoto machine or a piece of photographic printing paper on to which the negative has been placed. The percipient is not passive, but active. He is stimulated by such elements of the impression as form, movement, and content, as well as by all of the emotional associations he has at the time. He may be compared to a dreamer or some sleepy person looking at shadows on the wall. What he sees there are projections from within himself.

There is a similarity between a telepathic percipient and a subject in the Rorschach test. A series of ten ink blots was devised by the Swiss psychiatrist, Hermann Rorschach. The subject looks at each one of these ambiguous figures and tells what he sees in it, what it might or could be. What he sees is dependent upon the forces within himself. In this way he reveals the structure of his own personality. We are interested in this test as a clue to the conditions under which telepathic communication takes place. It is possible that good or bad reception is related to the character structure of the percipient and to his needs and motivation at the particular moment. In the telepathic experiment the composition of the target, too, is naturally of some consequence.

The subject in the telepathic experiment responds to more than one aspect of the impression. His perception tends to organize itself in conformity with his conscious and unconscious needs and drives as well as his background of experiences. Some aspects of the target stimulate intellectual reactions, others, emotional reactions. No two telepathic subjects respond alike to the same target. No two targets seem to affect the same subject in the same way. In many of our experiments two percipients were used. In one of these the target was the jacket of an elaborately decorated and colored travel folder displaying many symbols and aspects of Egyptian culture (Fig. 23). Mrs. M. responded emotionally to the snake, which became the dominant element in her perception. She also had an impression of the colors, "green, black, red." Mr. D., on the other hand, did not perceive the snake at all, or if he did, he repressed it or pushed it out of awareness. He merely noted, "pagoda" and "gondola."

In another instance we see a combination of movement and emotional elements. The target was a picture of monkeys (Fig. 24). The percipient, Mr. B., said, "I see an animal, jaws, its fangs, a gorilla, it is like a pair of pliers before gripping." He drew the pliers and reported that he had become first conscious of the element of movement. A similar example is the perception of a child's drawing (Fig. 25) in which the feeling tone is linked with an awareness of movement. The same factors seem to have been involved in the transmission of the idea of fire. The agent, Mr. B., locked himself in his photographic laboratory in complete darkness. He rubbed a little bar of ferro-cerium against a small piece of metal. There were sparks. I was the percipient, and I reported the following: "Mr. B. is playing with matches. One of the matches has caught fire. A white bar." Then I drew three matches lying one against the other. In

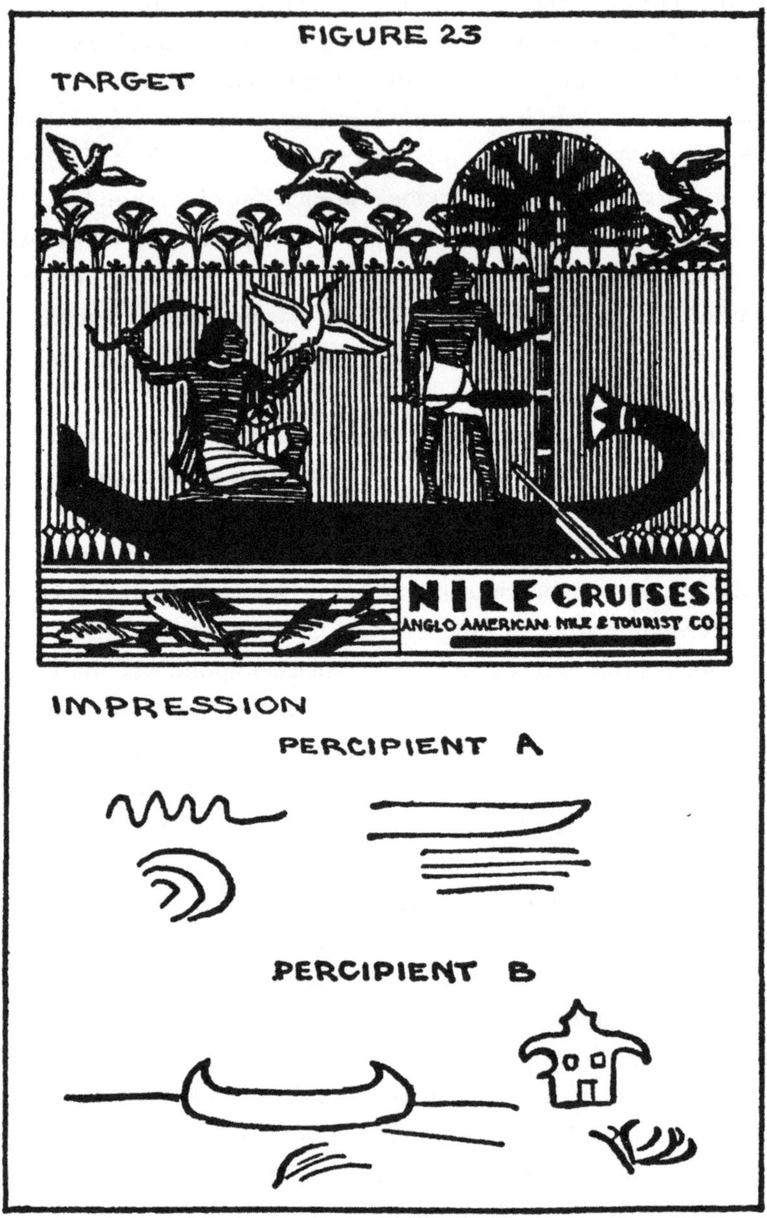

this connection it may be noted that Sinclair offers an interesting and detailed discussion of fire in telepathic communication.[2]

At this point I should like briefly to touch upon the question of color. In a number of our experiments the targets were colored, e.g., Fig. 23 and Fig. 24. In normal perception, color usually arouses some degree of affect or emotion.

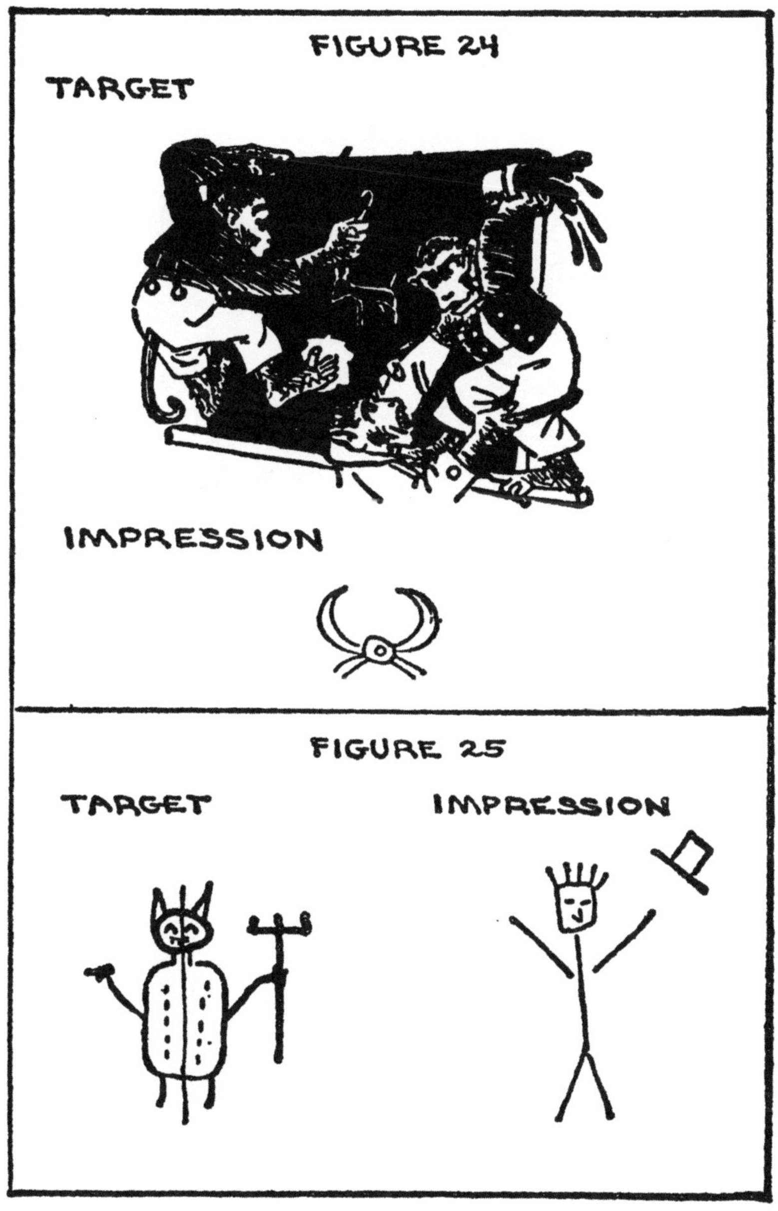

In paranormal perception the effect of color in the target varies; some percipients do not seem to respond to it at all. Although we do not know how color is transmitted, it is, nevertheless, perceived often independently of form. There is little of relevance to be found in the literature on parapsychology. Experiments dealing with the problem of color in telepathy are lacking. I have reported a few cases and discussed elsewhere the psychological theories relating to color.[3] I believe the phenomenon of contrast merits attention in this connection (see Fig. 15 and Fig. 21).

I IMAGINATION

IN SOME OF the experiments, dynamic elements seem to disappear. Instead of influencing each other, as in the process of condensation, or manifesting themselves directly in other forms, these elements seem to get lost in associated memories. We shall see this happen repeatedly in the cases described later. In all probability elements of the impression stimulate certain memory traces and expand themselves in that part of the process. It is the memory that has been excited and not the elements of the impression that comes to consciousness.

A drawing of butterflies against the sun was used as a target (Fig. 26). The percipient gained the impression of a rising sun with spreading rays. His thoughts did not stop here, however, and he began immediately to create an entire scene which resulted in a drawing of Napoleon at Austerlitz. Sometimes there is an imaginative elaboration of an impression correctly received as in the case of the photograph of the Grecian temple. The percipient drew it more ornately and in greater detail (Fig. 27).

The impression of the latent image excites the imagination and the memories of the percipient. These are confused and an interpretation results that frequently is highly original. It is possible that this process in telepathy has some relation to creative imagination in daily life. Perhaps telepathy plays a real role in the imaginative processes of most people, but an awareness of it is lost among the personal associations that it invokes. This is in line with my feeling that we are always dreaming, whether we are awake or asleep. On the whole, we remain unaware of our dreams. It may be that the telepathic message finds the means for expressing itself in those rare moments when our sense-centeredness lapses long enough for our dreams to come through.

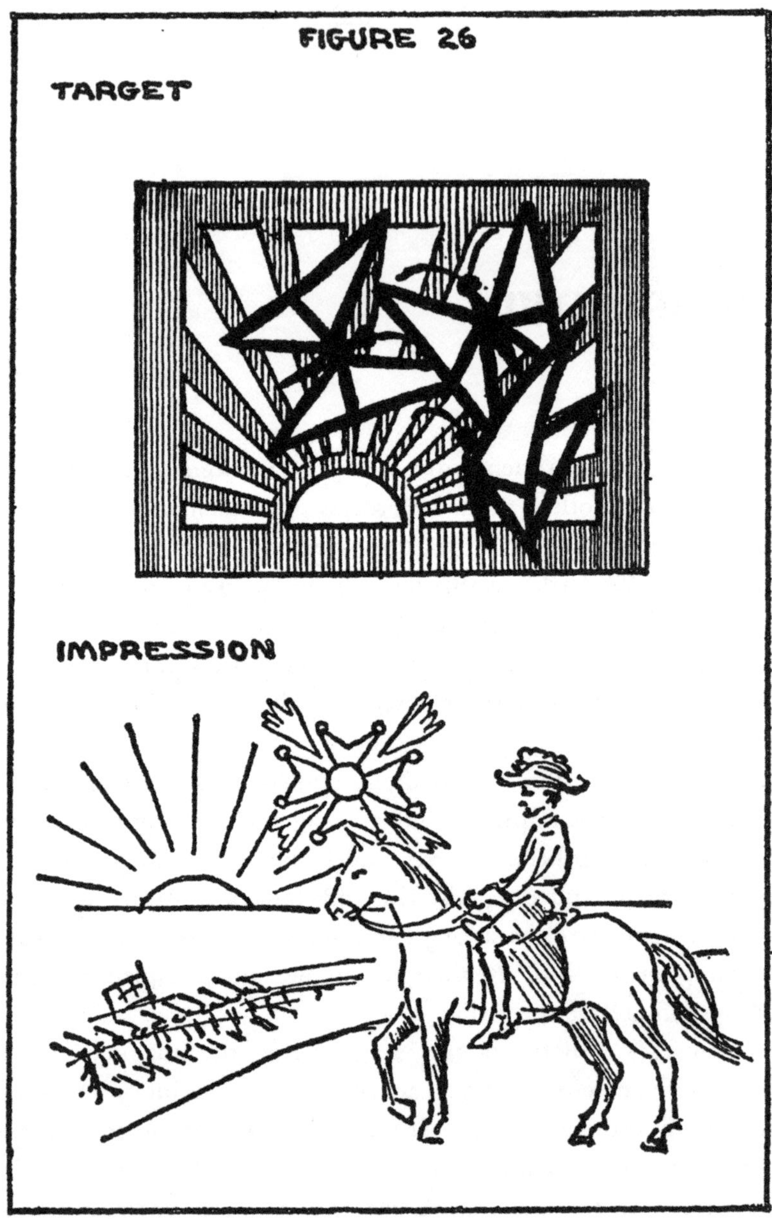

Conscious imagination is a negative force in telepathic communication. The purposeful attempt on the part of the percipient to use his imagination to gain the telepathic impression seems to hinder success. My experience runs contrary to the opinion of those who hold to psychic parallelism as a device for explaining telepathy away; they would have us believe that two people think

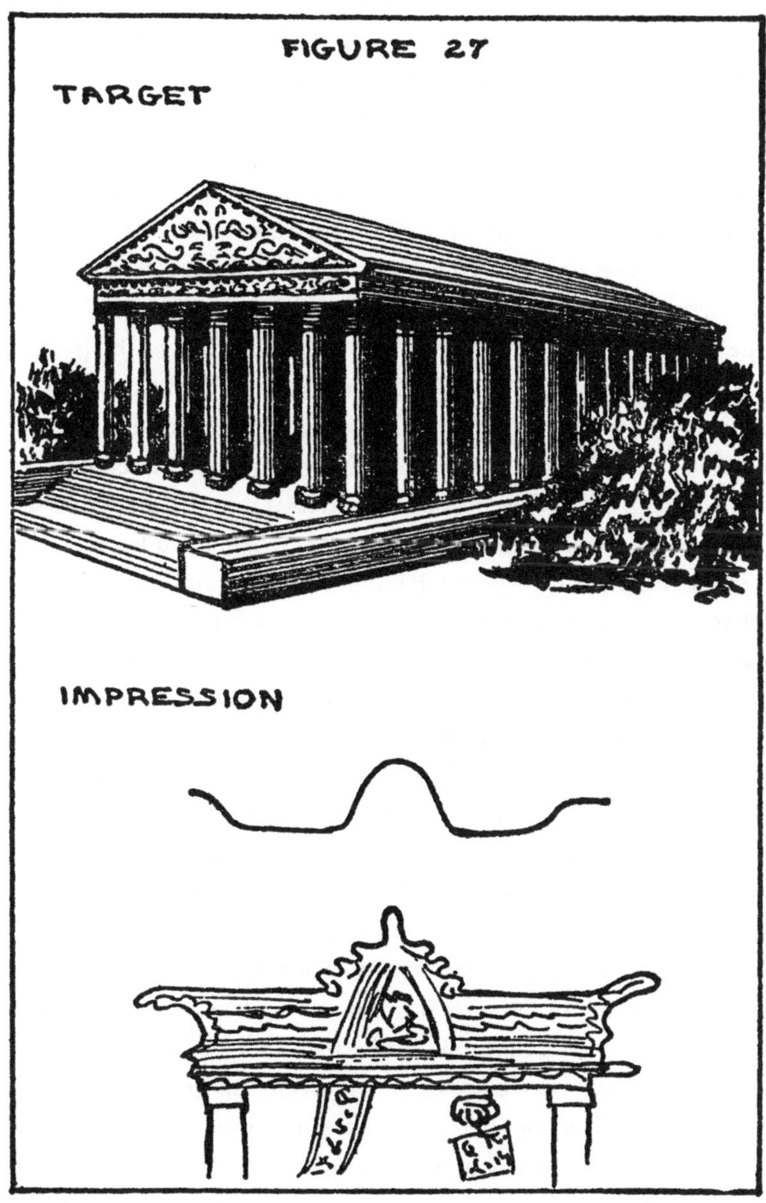

along parallel lines and simultaneously have the same thoughts, thus getting along without the operation of telepathy.

Under experimental conditions if the percipient and the agent share a common set of experiences the telepathic process will be influenced adversely. The telepathic impact may arouse in the percipient a whole chain of associations if any part of it is touched upon by the agent in the transmission of the target. Our experiments tend to show that telepathy is facilitated when the agent and the percipient scarcely know each other. Admittedly the very opposite seems to be true when telepathy occurs spontaneously in life situations. In this connection, however, we must not overlook the extremely valuable and suggestive work of Stuart, who reported several studies in the paranormal perception of drawings or pictures. He found, under experimental conditions, that "closely related pairs (twins, married couples, and engaged couples) gave significantly positive results" in contrast with the scores of unrelated pairs.

One of our experiments serves as a good illustration of the problem under consideration. The target was a pattern of angles, over the center of which was fixed a wavy white band of paper. The percipient wrote down the following impression: "union—marriage—procession—banners."[1] Then she drew one of the banners (Fig. 28). What possibly occurred is that the telepathic signal associating the angles with banners was received. It remained latent and gradually aroused the ideas of procession, wedding, marriage, and union. It was this last idea that first arose into consciousness and brought the associations along in reverse order. Certainly the meaning of these associations is highly personal. It serves no purpose to suppose that this chain of associations was inspired by something that happened in the immediate past of the percipient or by a recent exchange of ideas between the agent and percipient. Nor is it a matter of telepathic coincidence. The telepathic impact on a recent memory that is still conscious is too weak to come through. It seems to me that recent memories may, at times, even be inhibited by the telepathic impact and that more remote and forgotten memories are more easily awakened.

I do not wish to leave the impression that the telepathic impact excites the memory directly. In my opinion it occurs through what Abramowski calls the emotional potential of sensations, and what I call the dynamic subconscious. If the telepathic impact of a square acted directly upon the conscious memory, the result should be a complete square and not four right angles (see Fig. 2). The latent image takes form at an unconscious and almost impersonal level. A photograph of the percipient was once used as a target, and the percipient described the photograph in detail without recognizing himself.

Our experiments have led me to believe that the total personality is made up fundamentally of attitudes. These attitudes constitute the basis of all thinking and feeling. They are what Bergson calls "dynamic patterns." These dynamic patterns are the result of all past experiences and perceptions. As we approach each new experience or each new perception, these dynamic patterns

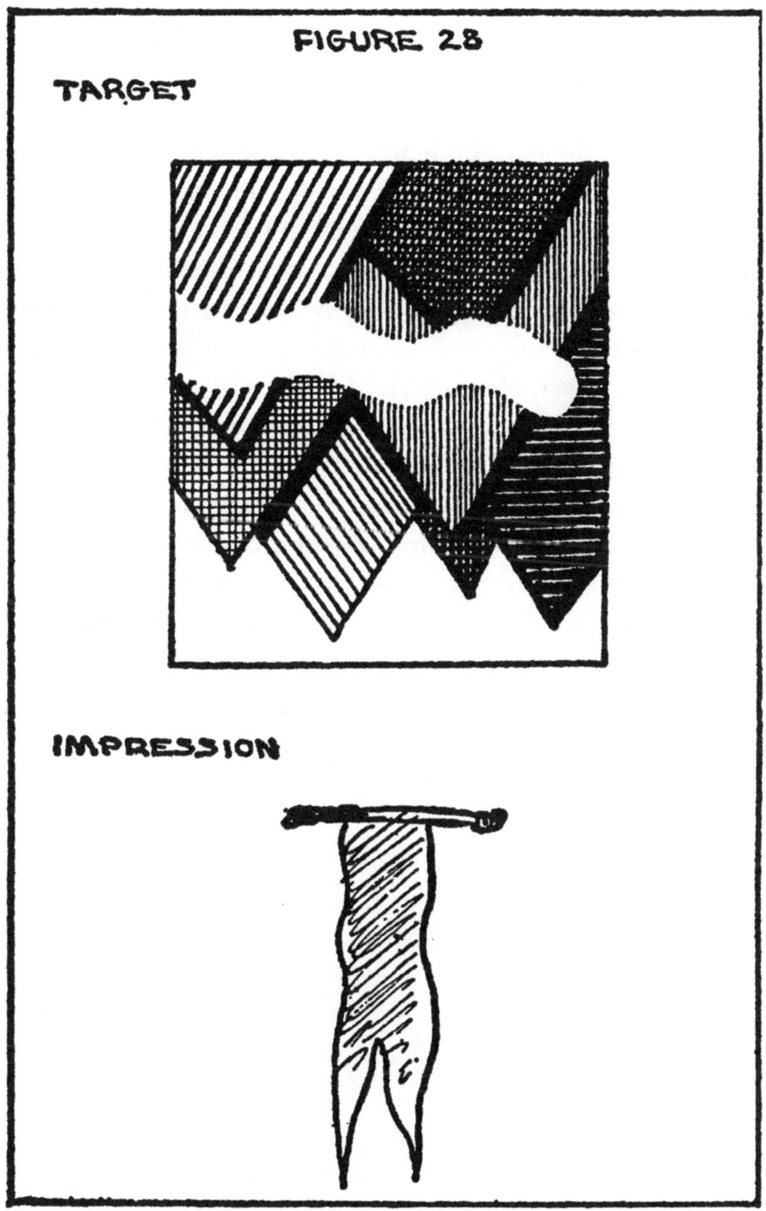

are aroused. The principle is essentially the same for a telepathic impression. When the telepathic impression is received by the percipient, the dynamic pattern which he acquired through normal perception of the same or similar object is reactivated. The mimetic pattern may take the form of thoughts, emotions, or bodily attitudes. Something analogous to what happens when the percipient draws the telepathic impression may be seen when the handwriting expert assumes the posture of the person whose handwriting he is attempting to analyze. This kind of identification with another person by mimicking his expressive movements is common among so-called primitive people. There are cases reported by anthropologists in which a sorcerer seeking to discover a thief will automatically take on the posture and play the role of the thief, and by retracing his steps follow a course leading directly to him. This process may be related to the question of empathy, that is, putting oneself into another's place.

Our studies reveal the fact that the receiver of a telepathic impression does not respond to the impression as if the object were being seen for the first time. The telepathic percipient of a rectangle, for example, is not in the same state, nor does he have the same attitude as the person who has never before seen a rectangle. He brings to it all of his past experience with rectangles. He now functions, not in terms of total perception, but in accordance with the processes already discussed which seem to affect telepathic communication. He may not see a rectangle at all, but the elements of a rectangle, such as the right angles, or he may even be affected primarily and exclusively by a tactile impression.

I TELEPATHY AND LANGUAGE

TELEPATHY HAS CERTAIN similarities to other forms of communication. In the normal exchange of ideas, language cannot function without sounds, gestures, alphabet, and writing, or other linguistic apparatus. In telepathic communication the mediating factor between the agent and the percipient is the unconscious.

Occasionally body gestures accompany the telepathic impression. These may be due to the inner movements through which ideas express themselves. These movements are quite frequently unconscious, as in the case of sensations which are transformed into and manifested through other senses. For example, sounds are sometimes transposed into ideas of movement. In one of our experiments we see the transformation of a tactile sensation into a visual image. The target was a tightly bandaged finger (Fig. 29). We did not warn the percipient in advance that we were not using a drawing. He had been accustomed to drawings as targets. His telepathic impression of the bandaged finger was "a tied-up bundle of twigs." He received no impression of the sensation of pain. Still another case illustrates this process of transposition. We were working with a special sensitive who usually verbalized her associations. First I asked her to describe in words what I had in mind. I went into another room where I looked at a simple drawing of an acute angle (Fig. 30). Her responses were, "a cowl," "Capdenac" (the name of a small village in France), and "cape." She was then asked if she could draw her impression, and she immediately made a figure with many acute angles. There is little doubt that the use of language can cause difficulty in receiving a telepathic impression, because the medium of exchange in telepathy is not language.

Telepathy is a means of communication without words. When language is used, it is highly symbolic, as in dreams, and the impressions are frequently

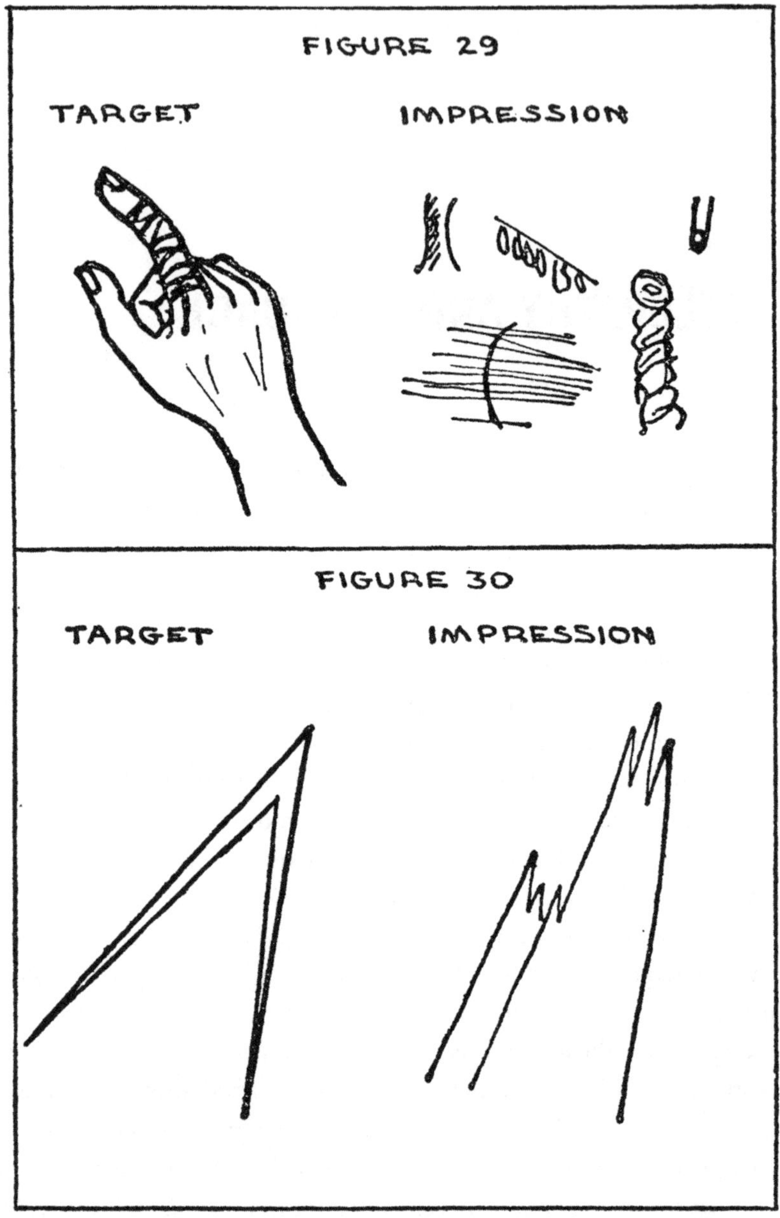

condensed into linguistic symbols that conceal the basic telepathic message. We have already noted how a child comes to associate a single word with his global perception. He would be hard put to do it if he were asked to analyze all of the sensations associated with the word he used to describe his perception. The global, syncretic perception is the frame of reference, or matrix, which binds together the many analytic elements contained in the impression. The child learns only much later the many subtle nuances and intellectual and emotional values attached to words.

In the foreword to an interesting recent study of spontaneous drawings of children, Nolan D. C. Lewis, the American psychiatrist, points out the symbolic character of this form of communication. He says, "The design like its contents has a special personal significance, although it uses a universal language which at certain levels is understood by all. The combinations are largely under the dominance of an unconsciously determined pattern of elements characteristic of phantasies, dreams,[1] childish beliefs and impressions, primitive associations, odd, free and conditioned associations, memories and assortments of free images."[2]

The telepathic percipient receives the agent's global impression as a syncretic pattern. It is the percipient who performs the synthesis of the analytic data that he, himself, discovers there. All perception takes place within a psychological organization that antedates the human acquisition of language. It is worth considering whether primitive means of communication existed in early man before the development of language.[3] We may ask the question, also, whether thought depends upon expression. It is my conviction that thought may exist without language and that telepathic impressions may be perceived without expression. In its most primitive form telepathy may produce coenesthetic disturbances, that is, sensations arising within the vital organs, including sensations of a depressing type; it may give rise to fits of weeping, vague presentiments or premonitions, confusions or disorientations, and the choice of one direction over another. All of these may be of paranormal origin at times, from our point of view.

In the preceding sections I have attempted to raise certain problems concerning the relationship between thought and language and between perception and memory. I cannot subscribe to the point of view of many psychologists that there is no thinking without language. Whenever we perceive an object in the world about us, we do not see it as it is in fact. We modify it by drawing associations from our memory. At the same time, there is much in a situation that we frequently overlook. What impresses us as well as what we miss can be understood only in terms of the dynamic patterns, conscious and unconscious, that constitute the human personality.

Telepathy is dependent upon memory. It would be impossible to receive a telepathic communication and to understand it without having had some prior experience with the conception it contains. Just as in a dream, a newly created image may seem to have no relation to experience. This is the result of dream work. Further analysis always reveals that the image is created out of elements deriving directly from experience. My feeling is that unexpressed thoughts do exist in the unconscious and that they are communicable. As a matter of fact, unconscious thought is most effectively transmitted. In the unconscious, thought is dynamic. When it becomes conscious, it loses much of its energy. It is "the end of the secret," as Binet-Sanglé is so fond of calling it. In his work he gives numerous historical examples of "secrets" being discovered paranormally; for example, Joan of Arc's intuitive recognition of Charles VII, disguised and hidden among his courtiers. Von Jorres cites the many saints who had the faculty for gaining knowledge of subliminal, unexpressed thoughts. He tells of the famous Curé of Ars who could discern "secret mortal sins." The student of parapsychology armed with the techniques of depth analysis may find the study of this class of paranormal experience fruitful.

Lévy-Bruhl pointed out that the telepathic image resembles the sign language of deaf mutes and of primitive people. Its characters are like those to be found in the words of primitive language. The cognitive and emotional elements of what they wish to express are blended. Feelings as well as formal and logical meanings are conveyed. I know of examples of such forms found not only in primitive language but also in the neologisms (newly coined words) of children and schizophrenics. Among beginners in telepathy, if what is perceived seems illogical and irrational, the chances are greater that it is a hit than when the percipient seems consciously to restrict himself to the specific names of concrete persons, places and things. The sense or meaning of a telepathic communication is generally symbolic, not literal.

Tyrrell has said: "The conscious experience of the percipient, whether it takes the form of a vision or a voice or a dream or an impulse, is a *created symbol,* which stands for the telepathic event. It is not the telepathic event itself, but is a signal created to inform the conscious mind that telepathy has occurred. That is why telepathic information is so often partly wrong. The symbolic signal may contain extraneous matter. It is a creation, just as a dream is a creation, contrived by some subliminal factor in the personality; and that factor has a strong dramatic sense and is not above elaborating and embroidering the signal it creates."[4]

Professional sensitives have at their disposal not only a basic perceptive talent but everything acquired by man since the development of language as well. They combine dynamic factors, elements of movement and emotion, with memories impregnated with intellectual concepts. Professional sensitives occasionally have brilliant successes. They also suffer amazing failures, probably because they let the logic of their cognitive processes enter into the description of what they cannot compare with the original. In experimenting with the telepathic communication of drawings, especially with new subjects, one has the feeling of being present at the dawn of human thought that expressed itself only in rhythm, gesture, and primitive dance. All of this is extremely suggestive for studies in the origin of language.

I TELEPATHY AND THOUGHT

WHAT IS THOUGHT? The process of thinking, which seems so simple and familiar to us, is actually a complex matter still open to argument and experiment.

Henri Piéron in his study, *Le Cerveau et la Pensée,* published by Alcan in 1923, introduces memory into the process of thought: "In its elementary form, thought represents nothing more than the successive evocation, by means of mnemonic mechanism, of sensory impressions of images, more or less completely revived. . . . One individual will think chiefly with the coordinating centers of visual images; another will express his thought in speech; still another will listen to his inner thought as if to speech, using solely auditory and verbal images. . . ."

Watson, in his studies on behaviorism, categorically states: "Thought is linguistic behavior."

Our telepathic experiments are concerned with an elementary form of thought. Let us try to discover if what is transmitted agrees with these definitions.

A second question arises from our studies: Is thought dependent upon language? Experiments seem to demonstrate that thought can be communicated independently of words. More important still, from the psychological point of view, the substratum of thought is revealed in telepathic communications. Our experiments have usually employed pictorial representations as the object or "target." But what, in fact, is communicated? Let us attempt to ascertain if the communication is composed of mental visual images—word-pictures, in effect.

A drawing is not a thought; it represents a thought. It is a thought objectified and, therefore, becomes *the thought of a drawing:* this is the object or target of mental communication. Since the drawing is a modification of a surface in space, it is, in the opinion of some, a source of paranormal sensitivity. The telepathic communication of drawings, like clairvoyance in the matter of drawings or objects, is more fragmentary than that of mental images. The details are what attract every percipient; rarely is the agent's idea evoked by his drawing. The same holds true of a thought expressed by a written word: it becomes the thought of a graphic representation, another drawing. Likewise a word pronounced at a great distance is not a pure thought, but a thought attached to sounds and which, by *clairaudience* (to coin a term) can be the object or target of a paranormal perception.

A mental image may be something quite different. It is certainly not an idea, but rather the representation of an idea under the apparent form of a vague projection on a mental screen.

The latent memory is considered by physiologists as a neuronic inscription, which becomes thought only at the instant when it attaches to itself some more or less conscious elements. The images of motion picture films projected on a screen, the images on the retina, and even their impact on the optic centers are not thought. Their diffusion in the memory awakens a multitude of recollections and emotions and ideas. *Apperception* occurs after the sensorial stimulus has passed through the memory.[1]

Communication of Symbols

In several experiments we found it possible to communicate signs, abbreviations, letters standing for words, and other types of symbols. In one of these experiments, the symbol was "S.O.S." I was the agent separated from the percipient by several rooms on different floors of a house. Privately I wanted to associate this symbol in an unusual way; not to the normal maritime distress signal, but to the atomic bomb and explosive fire. For this reason I had painted the letters with a black compound of uranium—mostly carbide.

The percipient drew a picture of a bird with wings spread, and wrote, in French, *Oiseau de feu* (Fire-bird), adding, *Oise S,* indicating the Oise prefecture and river of northern France, the S designating its southern portion, followed by "the sound ssszz." Evidently the percipient perceived simultaneously the shape of the letters and the hissing sound associated with the emotive idea attached to it. This constitutes telepathic communication (because of the idea of fire), rather than clairvoyance. However, it its difficult to interpret the exact results of an attempt to communicate a pictorial representation, either written or drawn. The percipient may quite well have perceived the symbol "S.O.S.";

but then, as the group of letters emerged into the conscious mind, the combination of letters became dissociated, fragmenting, as Abramowski has observed, "into its parts, the intellectual representation and the portion containing a fundamental emotional tone." I myself have observed such a dissociation when making an effort to remember a forgotten word.

Communication of Words

Abramowski, who experimented almost exclusively with words,[2] often interprets the results of his experiments in favor of clairvoyance.

Lombroso describes an experiment in which the word "teeth"* was used. The percipient wrote: "D, eye, butterfly wings, indented, dented (as in lace), teeth."**

Binet-Sanglé describes an experiment in which the Latin word *Amor* was selected; it is not clear whether it was spoken or written. The percipient received *"Marier"* (marry).

Miles and Tamsden describe an experiment in which the word selected was *slug.**** The percipient reported "Lemon sole," and then said, "It crawls, it is sticky. Ah, it is a slug!"****

A proper name "Phelip" was chosen. This was perceived as "Blé, Bel, Phe, Phelip, Philip, Philippines."

One of the most significant proofs that clairvoyance can vitiate telepathic experiments with written messages is to be found in experiments reported by Ossowiecki.

In this connection, an interesting result was obtained with the inscription *Non* in French, signifying *No* in English, a negative prefix. It was paranormally read as "a number of three digits, its central one being a zero."

In experiments carried out over a period of twenty-two years, Dr. Osty encountered but one subject able to detect a thought "selected and represented mentally." Usually the word was written on a piece of paper, for the purpose of subsequent control of the experiment. Under these conditions, some thirty successes were obtained, by dermography, with Madame K. An observation that I was able to make with the same sensitive, Madame K., leads me to believe that telepathy played a large role.

---

* Dents.

** D, oeil, ailes de papillon, dentelées, dentelles, dent.

*** Limace.

**** Limande. Ça rampe, c'est gluant. Oh, c'est une limace.

My personal experiment with Madame K. was carried out on the 10th October, 1928. Mr. Besterman of the Society for Psychical Research of London and I had come to the clairvoyante for the first time. Mme. K. asked me to think of my wife's Christian name—which is Germaine. I looked her in the eyes and she wrote: "C." Then she wrote "K," and finally "G." But she could not give the Christian name. Believing she might have better success with Mr. Besterman, she said I had only to tell him in a low voice the name of my wife, which he would then write on a piece of paper, all this to be done in her absence. She left the room, while I murmured the name and Mr. Besterman wrote it on a piece of paper which he folded twice and kept in his hand.

Madame K. returned, looked at Mr. Besterman and said, "Ganriette," to our great astonishment. The word was a combination of two names, Germaine and Henriette, which was the name of Mr. Besterman's wife, of whom he was not consciously thinking at the time, and whose name he had not written. This seems an instance of telepathic communication, or a fusion of telepathy and clairvoyance.

The responses of Madame K. recall the case described long ago by Alphonse Karr, in *Le sommeil magnétique expliqué par le somnambule Alexis* published by Dentu in 1856. "Someone gave the clairvoyant, Alexis, a paper folded several times and asked him to read what it contained. After some long hesitations, he said: 'I cannot read, because the person who gave me this paper did not write it herself. She had it written by a child who is here and the child wanted, at first, to write his name, then they made him write another word, and the name of the child is mixed up in my eyes with the word that was written.' They asked him, 'Well, can you see the name of the child?' And he answered, 'Oh, yes, he's called Charles.' Which was exact."

Communication of Whole Sentences Merely Thought

The extraordinary case cited by Carl du Prel,[3] which was considered typical of thought transmission before the work on clairvoyance carried out by Rhine, has not the same value today. In effect, Carl du Prel, without uttering a word, wrote on a piece of paper, "Baron von Schrenck-Notzing will read the poem, *Le coup du matin,* in silence and at a distance." The poem filled two printed pages. The clairvoyante was told that she would be questioned in regard to the poem, and then entered a trance state. Upon awakening, she was questioned about her dream. She recounted her dream in but a few words, which closely conformed to the text. Her description indicates that what most impressed her in the poem were images of movement. This seems to be an instance of thought communication, not clairvoyance, similar to the "Book-Tests,"* now well known, and the readings in a closed book successfully carried out by the clairvoyant, Alexis Didier.

In a memoir addressed to Cuvier and the Académie des Sciences in 1835,[4] Dr. Barrier, a provincial physician from Privas, cites his experiment with a young ecstatic, Euphrasie Bonneau, commonly called Euphrasine:

"She was so gifted in divining the thought of the person in rapport with her that she entered into a very sustained conversation with facility. In the course of one such conversation, her interlocutor did not speak aloud but expressed his thought *mentally.* On the occasion of my second visit, I found Euphrasine in deep trance, her body rigidly arched, supported only by her head and heels resting on the floor. More than twenty persons surrounded her, all of them maintaining a religious silence. I drew near, put myself in rapport, silently said good-day to the patient, concentrating on remaining silent and *without moving my tongue or lips.* 'Good-day, Dr. Barrier,' she replied. Mentally I put another question: 'When will you come to La Voutte?' To this she replied: 'As soon as possible.'"

Dr. Barrier now asked Madame Bonneau, the mother of Euphrasine, to try. After he had put her in touch with the ecstatic, Madame B. silently proposed to her daughter a walk to Cous next day. To this Euphrasine replied, "No, not to Cous, but to Alissas! To Alissas, I tell you!"

Conversations of the same order continued with a cousin and others present.

Commenting on this séance, Ochorowicz underscores the fact that "In conversations such as this, the agent does not speak."

Now, the mere perception of a "good-day," a verbal gesture of politeness that one carries out without reflecting, since it is barely a thought, is of slight import. But the sentence, "When will you come to La Voutte?" is a thought that is rather complex; and it was followed by other sentences to which the subject replied exactly as if the words had been spoken aloud and heard.

Communication of Thought Contained in a Word, Pronounced Aloud, But Beyond the Subject's Understanding

The following example is, again, drawn from the experience of a mesmerizer, Dr. Alexandre Bertrand:[5]

* For a succinct account of the "Book-Tests" see the article "Charles Drayton Thomas, Pioneer Researcher," in *Tomorrow*, Summer 1961, pp. 89-99.

"A poor and uneducated woman, not even able to read, was yet capable, when under hypnosis, of understanding the meaning of words whose significance was unknown to her in the waking state." This woman explained in the most accurate and confident way the meaning of the word *encephalon,* which Dr. Bertrand suggested to her. "This is a phenomenon," comments the Doctor, "which if not considered the result of mere chance—as difficult to admit as the very faculty it supposes—can only be explained by recognizing that this woman read in my own thoughts the meaning of the word upon which I had questioned her."

In *Histoire du Somnambulisme* by Gauthier published by Dentu in Paris in 1842, we find a more precise detail of this experiment.

"I was far from expecting a satisfactory reply when I saw her rise up on her bed, bring her hands to her forehead, and slowly trace, with a finger, a circular line round her head going from the base of the nose and passing behind the occiput. . . . I admired the expedient she used to show me she had understood."

Communication of a Command Given in a Tongue Unfamiliar to the Subject

The possessed Ursuline nuns of Loudun understood the thoughts of their exorcisers.[6] Numerous cases were cited, all well observed. I will quote Ochorowicz.[7]

The brother of the King Gaston, Duc d'Orléans, certified on the 11th of May, 1635, that a nun obeyed a command he had given mentally without uttering a word or making a sign. The possessed nun had approached Father Elysée and kissed his right hand—that was the order issued by the Duke, in thought only.

"Father Surin affirmed on his sacred word that the possession was quite evident, and swore before God and the Church that more than two hundred times the demons had revealed to him very secret things hidden in his mind or on his person."

The Ursuline nuns were exorcised twice a day for seven years. We know what Father Surin also declared: "I felt the devil passing from the body of the possessed person into mine. . . ."

Replies to Questions Put in a Language Unknown to the Subject

The exorcisers put questions in Latin to the demons (there was a complete hierarchy of them), and the nuns replied correctly in that language. However, it was quite possible that they knew some Latin, since they heard it spoken daily in their presence.

Far more convincing are the following examples cited by Ochorowicz:

"Monsieur Launay de Barillé asserted that, during a trip he made to Loudun, he spoke to the nuns in the language of certain savages of America, where he had lived, and that they replied to him quite relevantly in French."

Unfortunately, we are given none of the details of this conversation. If the gentleman merely said to the nuns, "Good-day, how are you," which is probable, the tone of voice alone would reveal the meaning. But there are other instances:

"The Bishop of Nîmes, having questioned the nuns in Greek and German, was able to communicate in either one or the other language. Employing Greek, he commanded Sister Claire to *raise her veil* and to *kiss the iron grille* at a designated spot; she obeyed, and did many other things he asked her to do. Which caused the prelate to say openly that one must be either an atheist or a fool not to believe in 'possession by demons.'"

"Some gentlemen of Normandy certified that they had interrogated Sister Claire de Sazilly, in Turkish, Spanish, and Italian, and that she had replied quite aptly in French."

If occurrences of this type could be observed, experimented with, and studied today, the question which preoccupies us—the independence of thought from language—might approach solution. In the case of the nuns of Loudun discussed above, we do not have the transmission of words, or of words assembled to form sentences; what seems to be transmitted is the thought itself.

A mesmerizer of modern times, Charles Lafontaine,[8] has reported a similar case:

"During my stay in Tours," he writes, "I mesmerized a clairvoyante to whom one spoke in Spanish, Latin, English, Portuguese, German, and Greek, and she replied in French to all the questions put in these diverse languages. But when someone asked her a question in Hebrew, the clairvoyante did not reply. I urged her to answer, asking why she did not, and she explained, 'The reason is simple. This gentleman speaks words to me but does not understand them. . . .' And in fact, the gentleman concerned admitted that he had asked an Israelite for the sentence in Hebrew, but had not remembered to ask its meaning."

We no longer deal with subjects possessed by demons, nor do we have ecstatics or clairvoyants at our disposition; our subjects are "metagnomes"—persons who, in psychic research, have been found to be especially sensitive percipients.

With these subjects, as Dr. Osty emphasized, the phenomenon of thought transmission manifests itself with amazing frequency. Thoughts, not words, are communicated. For, as Dr. Osty has declared, "These occurrences of thought transmission are so plentiful, and there is such a steady stream of them, that the contrast is striking when compared with the isolated words and phrases that the subjects, selected for their capabilities, are able laboriously to detect."

Dr. Osty was always more specifically interested in "the human side of the phenomenon of communication from mind to mind—of the hopes, desires, fears, worries, and anxieties of the vibrant human psyche in the midst of the animate and inanimate world."[9] Aside from the instances of thought communication carried out with subjects put into a receptive state, he also encountered instances of spontaneous communication—of remembered images, of Christian and family names, often by the interpretive use of a curious verbal symbolism.

Having had occasion to experiment for several years with one of these sensitives, a certain Madame B. (an amateur, not a professional), I was able to observe several times instances of mind to mind communication of this order. The thoughts I communicated were scientific; more precisely, in the technical field of chemistry, of which she knew absolutely nothing. In attempting and achieving this, I found myself in the situation of the old-time observers, for I was thinking in a language unknown to the percipient.

Communication of Ideas without Equivalent in the Vocabulary of the Percipient

Immediately before the séance, I had been professionally occupied in carrying out a chemical purification culminating in a white precipitate of high refractive index.

Madame B. used the ouija board for the consultation. She was the only one to touch it and I remained at a distance.

The ouija dictated: "He seems to clean elements that are not pure enough until the object is stripped. *Light vapors on the handle of his brush. Shining, lily-clear.*"

I asked what was meant by "lily-clear."

The reply was: "Very, very white."

The "brush" in question was a spatula which at a certain phase of the reaction became covered with a very shiny white deposit, a sign of the success of the operation.

In another séance the ouija dictated: "brushing." And it continued: "Horizontal and balancing movement. Manganese, increase the dosage, 1/3 profit."

The word "brushing" was inexact. The word could have been "threshing," to mix or stir. The mechanical mixer was something very special and I had not yet employed it to replace the spatula, but I was intending to do so. The balancing movement in the chemical operation was typical. Manganese is an exact transmission of a word. My experiment concerned a compound of manganese, of which I had the secret. The "increase of the dosage" in this product did yield 1/3 more, which was not obvious, but which I could have guessed. The sensitive percipient, Madame B., probably knew the word manganese, since she was an educated woman.

In still another séance, to express the chemical term "precipitated," the ouija employed an incorrect word, "induration" which, in the medical sense, means a hardening and incompletely expressed the idea; but Madame B. added the explanatory phrase, "that is to say, espousals."

Now, "espousals" is the expression alchemists employed for the idea of combinations of elements resulting in precipitation, or, as they put it, "the conjunction of male and female principles of bodies."

Upon arriving at the séance, I had been meditating on the possibility of using a retort in the chemical operation which would protect the mixture from air, keeping it in a gaseous atmosphere of carbon dioxide.

The sensitive indicated that she had received my thought when she said: "All the chinks blocked up, no air, no draught of air, no wind. You must not. Very dangerous, can't move about, protection by a gaseous layer."

The ouija then dictated: "Downy feathers."

The whole idea, an expression of the delicacy and lightness of those microscopic and fragile crystals, was penetrated when Madame B. added: "Something very delicate, rarefied, as fine as filaments. You need a tool to touch them. Tweezers impair. You need a minimum of contact. Proceed in another way, a horizontal silk spider-web will keep them in *suspension.*"

Here the correct chemical term was employed. The idea was particularly complex, and not a verbal or graphic image. "Very dangerous" was an overdramatization—common with sensitives—of the fear I had of seeing the precipitate become colored by the presence of oxygen. "Downy feathers" was a condensed image of the idea of air and the weightlessness of the precipitate. It was not verbalism, but a logical assemblage of ideas.[10]

In a perfect description of the life and character of one of my associates, Madame B. added, "You have more than a collaboration with him; your association is a *congrégat.*"

The night before, as I conversed with this associate, I had been thinking of the word "aggregate," borrowed from my chemical vocabulary. Now, the word *congrégat* is not a proper word in either French or English; it was invented outright and very correctly expressed what could have been said only in a paraphrase. Here we not only have an instance of telepathy of an idea, but also of a verbal form.

Madame B. normally had an excellent and vivid style and expressed herself very correctly; but, in her condition of semitrance she used such archaic terms as "espousals," or "niggardliness" instead of avarice, or neologisms having nothing to do with an interpretation of a telepathic message but which were the result of her condition of trance. For instance, I noted that she said "interferation" for "intervention," and "a beginner in power" for "unskillful." At the ouija board especially she no longer made use of the language-center of the brain and said, for example, "Nothing is written about true dreams," when she meant, "Nothing true has been written about dreams."

As if I were an exorciser, I asked the personality moving the ouija to tell me its name. The personality did not describe herself as a spirit, but replied what I had guessed: "It is my dear woman friend who has summoned herself."

I then questioned the medium as to what the ouija meant to say. She explained that "summoned herself" meant "came of her own accord," "called herself," or "communicated with herself."

These experiments and accounts demonstrate that the *unspoken thought* of an assemblage of letters, words, and phrases can be communicated from one mind to another. The meaning of a word not normally understood can be understood by communication of thought—even the meaning of a word pronounced in a language unknown to the percipient. Not only can the meaning of an isolated foreign word be transmitted, but a conversation can be carried on in which one of the interlocutors (the agent) does not speak out loud but merely thinks what he wishes to communicate. We have also noted the telepathic passage from mind to mind of abstract ideas and thoughts, the comprehension being expressed in metaphors when the terms of thought in the agent's mind are nonexistent in the vocabulary of the percipient.

It may be assumed that the communication of thought can be achieved independently of the usual spoken or written forms of expression. In the light of the experiments cited we may reconsider the question, "What relationship exists between the intellect and verbal expressions?" We have cited the opinions of Piéron and of Watson, to whom thought is not independent of language.[11]

According to Wundt, the origin of speech is linked to the origin of language-by-gestures; the word was at its beginning only a gesticulation. Dumas, in *Traité de Psychologie,* adds the observation that "Primitive societies and uneducated deaf-mutes reveal the possibility and sporadic persistence of a more primitive language, less arbitrary than oral language. This entails a kind of controlled gesture of the body, particularly of the hands, which develops into expressive phrases."

Lévy-Bruhl writes that this gesture language seems to be widespread throughout South America, where the Indians of different tribes do not understand each other's speech. They need and use a language of gesture to talk together—and they can talk thus for half a day, recounting all kinds of stories.

According to Sir Richard Paget, "Human thought begins when man acquires the ability to separate in his mind the items of his environment, giving to each a symbol apart from gesture. Before this stage is reached he does not speak, but moves the tongue in harmony with the hands. It is only at the stage where the same movement has invaribaly the same connotation that words appear."[12]

It seems that thought is built up from a substratum, based on conditioned reflexes and sensory elements, which give rise to simple mental symbols taking the form of images and of sounds; and then, finally, the form of words. It is very likely that articulated language, and much later written language, developed the intellectual faculties of man, the intellectual development corresponding with the richness and flexibility of the language. However, in the course of this development, man's primitive intuition has been weakened.

"With deaf-mutes, progress is visibly arrested in the third year, and the language of gesture subsequently constitutes an impediment to the development of thought, as compared with its growth in a normal child. Gesture is always equivocal and contributes to the syncretism and blurring of thought, which impedes the formulation of logical concepts. Moreover, the deaf-mute thinks in images always attached to a concrete object, which prevents his mind from liberating itself towards abstract thought."[13]

"When language is employed, thought has already entered a realm of logic. No sooner is an object perceived than it is named, and the name it evokes reacts upon the perception. Together the name and perception are drawn together into the realm of logical relationships—which to be exact, is the realm of words. The perception is intellectualized. But, for a long time in the development of man, language remained objectified."

"In primitive languages," states Lévy-Bruhl, "the tendency is to describe *form, contours, position, movement,* and *mode of action* of objects in space, rather than the perceived impression made on the mind by these objects. In short, the tendency is to describe what can be perceived and pictured. These languages try to make the plastic and graphic details correspond to what they try to explain."

The same characteristics may be observed in the telepathic transmission of drawings, which often contain deformations identical to those characteristics of the thought of children and primitive man.[14] An example of this is a telepathic experiment in which the agent held in his hand a small chart of the subway folded in two, and half opened; the percipient received a "bi-valve, a scallop." Ribot wrote "The Australian Aborigines call a book 'a mussel' because it opens and shuts like the bi-valve."[15]

In our experiments we have noted a certain confusion between giraffe and camel. A. Cramaussel wrote that "the child confuses . . . a swan with a giraffe or camel."[16] And we have discovered an identical confusion in ourselves—a lapse of memory, a slip of the tongue—during fatigue. For example, in 1943, in the course of a conversation regarding a daylight bombing, I was told that my interlocutors merely drew the dark blind of the window. I commented, "Like a giraffe." Realizing that I had made a slip, I glanced at my listeners to see what their reactions had been. They had not noticed. But after a pause I referred again to our conversation and admitted the lapse: "I meant to say, 'Like an ostrich.'" The connection was the length of neck, as with the child's confusing the camel with the swan.

In the form of observable objects we have the primary element of thought—quite independent of language. Here we have the Kantian quanta which Bergson revived and developed in a thousand ways.[17] But not all psychologists share these theories.

According to Dimier intelligence and language begin and develop simultaneously. Language is only one prerequisite for advanced thought. Thought itself has a rudimentary existence (always present, manifesting itself in telepathy), just as a certain musical sense existed before musical notation. It must not, therefore, be concluded that thought does not exist without the evolution of the word. This notion has been challenged not only by our telepathic experiments, but also in our usual manner of expression in words either written or spoken aloud.

This fact has not been overlooked by the psychologist C. Konczewski. "In general, creative thought is elaborated entirely in the depths of our being," he declares, "emerging from it into the conscious mind in suggestions and ready-made statements—the conscious mind merely selecting, controlling, and interpreting these manifestations, just as one revises and corrects a first draft when writing."[18]

The role of the conscious mind may be even more restricted. The expression of my thought in words surprises me as much as if the words had been spoken by someone else. We are incapable of recapturing a word "on the tip of the tongue"; we must wait until the subconscious sends the word to us. In dreams, a thought often expresses itself in visual images only. And, as we have already said, the process of thinking is not the same for everyone.

For William James, who was a visual thinker, a thought such as "The deck of cards is on the table" was an image he saw. This case corresponds closely to the definition Piéron gave: "In its elementary form, thought . . . is an evocation of sensory impressions. . . ."[19]

In purely psychological and nontelepathic experiments, when the percipient was addicted to kinesthetic imagery, the phrase "The infinite hovers over all things" brought the following reactions: the word "Infinite" impelled him to spit the word from his mouth and to follow it by body movements having no particular visual symbolism, whereas another percipient would probably have had a mental image of the celestial vault. At the word "hovers" he had the impression of suddenly extending his hands and bending forward. "All" (in French, *Tout*) represented a wide opening of the mouth, and a movement of embracing, his two hands reaching out to sweep all space and then returning to clasp in front of the body. "Things" gave the mental impression of a sudden and direct gesture of the hand, the index finger pointing ahead and down.

Another percipient, when asked what impression was given by the word "in," explained that it gave the impression of snuggling down into something, without knowing what that something could be. For the word "but" there was a feeling of a suspended motor attitude.[20]

As I set these words on paper, "It seems to me that I am justified in selecting a personal example," I note that they are dictated to me by a completely unconscious process which uses word symbols as dynamic conceptualizations to interpret inner states of mind.

I find in the phrase "it seems to me" vague memories of propulsive muscular hesitation on confronting events. Those words were followed by a decision which was favorable and expressed by the words "I am justified." "Selecting" reminds me of numerous experiences of fumbling. Something is being weighed; I say "weighed" because at that instant I had the mental image of a pair of scales.* I was weighing the arguments of others against mine, and the

---

* *pensare*, Latin, to think, means "to weigh."

result was a favorable egocentric balance, a process of possession expressing the value I attached to my own judgment: "A personal example."

In that short phrase, different springs of thought flowed together and gushed out in a single stream. The phrase was formed unconsciously; I chose and arranged one word and then another—as they passed through the memory center of the brain.[21] The words came to me and were strung together in the time it took to write them. What, then, is thought? How can psychologists and metapsychologists be brought into agreement on its definition?

Thought is, for me, an effect; the effect of a grouping of the mnemonic data (even present sensory perceptions), into the form of dynamic schemes, which naturally include traces of the graphic signs of words, of their sounds and combinations.

A state of awareness is surely the first prerequisite for thought. For, as we have shown, under certain conditions of ecstasy or trance thought may be reduced to an elemental awareness of existence, or of being, which is totally dissociated from all else.[22] It is this awareness that differentiates a savage from a calculating machine. But this awareness is not just a cognizant entity, a syncretism of disparate schema. This awareness empowers us to make choices and to organize our thoughts into logical concepts; it is this which distinguishes an Einstein from a savage.

Organization takes place backstage in the normal waking state of consciousness, where it assumes the guise of the mental images—visual or auditory—of an inner language. There is no rift at all between the data obtained in our telepathic experiments and psychological or even physiological data. The communication of thought suggests that this "taking cognizance," this coming into awareness can occur not merely in our own mind but in other minds as to the concepts, ideas, and thoughts that are being elaborated, especially if this awareness is not objectified in consciousness. It is in the percipient's mind that the agent's thought will emerge through the percipient's own dynamic schemes, memories, and ideas.

The argument we have just stated conflicts with a basic tenet of psychology, which maintains that "A thought cannot be transmitted from one consciousness to another. Exactly as the physician speaks of the impenetrability of matter, so the psychologist may speak of the impenetrability of minds."[23]

With such a fixed tenet, how can the psychologist grasp the arguments of the parapsychologist? There is a wide rift here, and a bridge must be found if the psychologist is to cross it.

CONCLUSION

EXPERIENCE WITH TELEPATHY over the years has dispelled for me all doubt of the existence of a paranormal faculty in human beings. There is general resistance against accepting as a fact a telepathic faculty in man. The psychological bases and implications of this resistance are discussed at length by Tyrrell in his most recent work.[1] I have come to believe that those who will try for themselves such experiments as I have attempted to introduce here with drawings will be convinced. For I am in agreement with Carington when he says: "I have no doubt at all that the drawings-technique as a whole, using any statistically valid method of assessment, is truly repeatable, in the sense that anyone who cares to do what I have done will obtain substantially the same results; though he may not, of course, if he elects to do something different."[2]

It is unfortunate that the results of scientific investigation are rejected *a priori* regardless of the care of the investigators and the number of controls, if they are in the field of parapsychology. In the main, however, I have been concerned here not with evidence for a telepathic faculty, but rather with the whole problem of mental imagery elucidated by our studies in the telepathic communication of drawings. The relation between paranormal and normal perception and the universality of certain psychological principles strengthen my conviction that we are dealing in the paranormal with natural effects, not with supernatural happenings.

The process of telepathy has not yet been defined in such terms as to attract the attention of the more mechanistically minded natural and social scientists. I do not feel that I have solved many of the problems and, in retrospect, I have probably raised more questions than I have answered. Parapsychology is a developing science and its terms as well as its elements are being rapidly redefined. I have used words that may have lent confusion instead of clarification, largely because some of the aspects are, in themselves, not too clear. My first impulse, for instance, was to reject the word "transmission" because in telepathy we are dealing with a two-way process. Interchange involves both sending and receiving. In fact, one person may act as both sender and receiver at the same moment.

I should like to propose for consideration a theory that I have been developing for some time concerning the personality of man. Consciousness seems to be the point of interaction between two dynamic worlds, the external field of stimulation giving rise to sense data, and the internal field arising from the electronic action of nerve tissue. Every sense perception is echoed by a dynamic alteration in the organization of the nervous system. A trace is left that remains unconscious, but its rhythm is, nevertheless, associated with memory images corresponding to perception. The first time we see an angle, for example, we are aware of having acquired a mental image of such a figure. At the same time, however, there is an unconscious acquisition of an associated pattern of nervous activity. The electrical energy of our nerve cells, if we may call it such, encounters the original figure of the angle on a three-dimensional plane and projects itself against it. There is an unconscious shock or impact which is registered by the nerve cells along with the visual perception of the angle. Should a child see for the first time a drawing of an angle instead of an object forming one, he would respond to it exactly as if it were a three-dimensional solid. The traces of ink have the same effect as the outline of the object itself. This may have some bearing on the origin of pure clairvoyance. Paranormal perception frequently does not distinguish between a drawing and a mental image of the object drawn. In some of our studies it could be seen that in paranormal perception the subject responded to a drawing as if it were a real object. The reverse was also to be found when the subject anticipating a drawing as the target responded to a real object as if it were a drawing. The vague and indistinct impressions that are received telepathically affect the nervous system in the same way as the normal perception of a three-dimensional object in space. In many ways the theory I am proposing is like certain contemporary hypotheses in physiological psychology.[3]

I am not subscribing here to the theory of cryptethesia of Richet or to that of the radiationists who believe that the perception is due to radiations given off from an object or a drawing. My emphasis is rather upon the percipient. The human being is dynamic, not the target. If there are any radiations, they must stem from him. It is my firm conviction that in the personality of the percipient we shall find what will prove most valuable for the understanding of paranormal manifestations. The percipient is the activator, the active agent who goes out of himself, so to speak, to receive the impression, rather than the passive apparatus upon which waves or radiations act. It is the impact, I believe, of the unconscious forces from within the personality of the percipient upon the target, whether the target be a person or a drawing or a thing, that activates memories and associated feelings within him. The nervous energy that is then brought into play may revive whole areas in the unconscious of the percipient on the fringe of the specific unconscious image of the target itself. It is as if a series of self-activating stimuli had been set off so that the first impact brings further chains of reaction and patterns of experiences involving intellectual and emotional components. These experiences originate in normal perception, for without the memory of prior experience, the telepathic impression would be unrecognizable and meaningless. It is only within the realm of the percipient's experiences that we can understand the telepathic message. He must draw upon his organized patterns of feeling and thinking to give meaning to what arrives from the unconscious.

The question of clairvoyance is sometimes raised when drawings, pictures or objects are used as telepathic messages. What is usually meant by clairvoyance is the direct paranormal perception of a target without the intermediation of an agent. There is some doubt in my mind that clairvoyance in this sense does occur. Even when sensitives ask for the opportunity to psychometrize,[4] that is, to have physical contact with an object or target, it seems more reasonable to suppose that the information is known to someone else who may act as an agent. The operation of telepathy, therefore, cannot be excluded. I have not overlooked the fact that the object or target plays a role of dynamic opposition to the forces arising from within the percipient as well as the agent. If this did not occur, the impression received by the percipient would be without shape or form. It should also be possible for sensitives to perceive an exposed but undeveloped photographic plate or a drawing made with water and leaving no trace on the paper. Experiments of this kind have not met with success.

In all paranormal communication, we must take into consideration the personality of the experimenter or agent. The telepathic impression is created in the percipient's mind, but in accordance with a theme or pattern originating in the agent's. The agent, in turn, may be stimulated by a picture, object, event or, as in our experiments, by a drawing. The personality of the agent is inextricably involved as part of the total situation that is to be perceived. The specific object or target is never approached without relationship to the agent who acts as a relay. Carington's experiments seem to have led him to expound a similar position. I believe that a pattern of electronic action in the agent, which is stimulated by an object, is able spontaneously and dynamically to stimulate a similar energy pattern in the percipient and to awaken in his consciousness associations of ideas connected with the object. The more dynamically the agent and the percipient participate in a telepathic experiment, the greater are the chances of success.

In general, our minds are strongly sense-centered, and we pay attention mainly to sensory data. We give little heed to stimuli arising from within ourselves. If experience in paranormal introspection could be provided, that is, if we could focus our attention upon inner stimulation and impressions, I believe a certain telepathic sensitivity might be developed. I have little evidence for this hypothesis, but its acceptance or rejection does not affect the reality of telepathy. In his book, *Mental Radio,* Sinclair offers some suggestions as to how our introspective capacity may be enlarged.[5]

The quantitative studies of such investigators as Rhine and Soal provide evidence of the existence of telepathy even for the most critical student. An objective evaluation of the data leaves little doubt that extrasensory perception is a human faculty. The quantitative proof to be found in the literature gives me a sense of confidence and assurance that my own qualitative studies are meaningful. To be sure, the number of successes in our experiments with nonprofessional subjects has been somewhat disappointing. On the other hand, such experiments as were considered failures provide no argument against the existence of telepathy. Moreover, the experiments counted as failures because the results do not seem to be acceptable as evidence may have been truly successful telepathic exchanges. In these cases the telepathic impression may have undergone such transformation and distortion in that part of the process from the unconscious to the conscious, that the perception was no longer recognizable when compared with the original. The distortion has the appearance of being purposeful and "deliberate." If we are unusually analytic, we may, at times, be able to penetrate the disguise.[6]

We tried working with different experimenters and with different subjects. We found that some experimenters always produced the same kind of distortion and some percipients always made the same kind of error with similar targets. Is there a common cause? There is so little known as yet about the structure and function of the human personality that we may come to ascribe such distortions and errors to dynamic factors in the participants rather than to the process of telepathic communication.

Before closing I should like to deal with a few specific cases bearing directly on these theoretical considerations. In some of our studies, targets of the same class were transmitted by different agents to the same percipient. Seventeen years had elapsed between the two trials using different agents and the St. Andrew's Cross as the target (Fig. 31). I was the percipient in both cases. You will note that each time my impressions were very similar (compare with Fig. 11). On another occasion, in 1926, the agent selected a flower as the target, and I had the impression that it was a kind of butterfly (Fig. 32). In 1927 the same agent, again by chance, selected a flower as a target, and I again made a somewhat similar drawing (Fig. 33). In 1925 a gruesome picture of a hanging man gave me the impression of "featherless wings, of fleshless bone" (Fig. 34). Two years later a drawing of a man reclining, lying as if lie were dead, came to me in the form of a drawing of a "shoulder blade newly stripped of flesh." (Fig. 35). The drawing of a desk lamp in 1935 (Fig. 36) and again in 1936 (Fig. 37) resulted in very similar impressions.

In 1926 a design of brightly colored triangles aroused in me a thirty-six-year-old forgotten memory. I later pursued the association and discovered an old photograph which formed the basis of this memory. It showed a group of people playing cards. The following year a very similar target, consisting of colored angles and circles, gave me the impression of playing cards. This particular case has implications that are worth further discussion. It had been conceived as a group experiment in which there were several percipients. One of the other percipients seemed to have been affected by my impression of a playing card, a heart. This process of mental contagion I have discussed on many other occasions. Now in the case of Mr. D., who picked up my impression of the playing card, the telepathic impact was associated with the idea of a stained-glass window of a cathedral; he drew first a flying buttress and then a gargoyle. A third percipient, Mr. A., was in turn influenced by the gargoyle. He associated it with a Japanese monster. What is most striking is that Mr. A. and I both used the same words in expressing our impressions, *"dessin vermiculé"* (wormlike drawing).

I am not going to take this occasion to enter into the problem of mental contagion.[7] It seems to work among several percipients even when they are separated by great distances. It is my feeling that psychological accord leads to psychological harmony and results in polypsychic fusion. People who work closely together and are highly motivated in achieving results in a group enterprise frequently share unconsciously many thoughts. These unconscious communications are telepathic in nature and take the form of mental contagion. For us, this is another bit of qualitative evidence for the existence of telepathy.

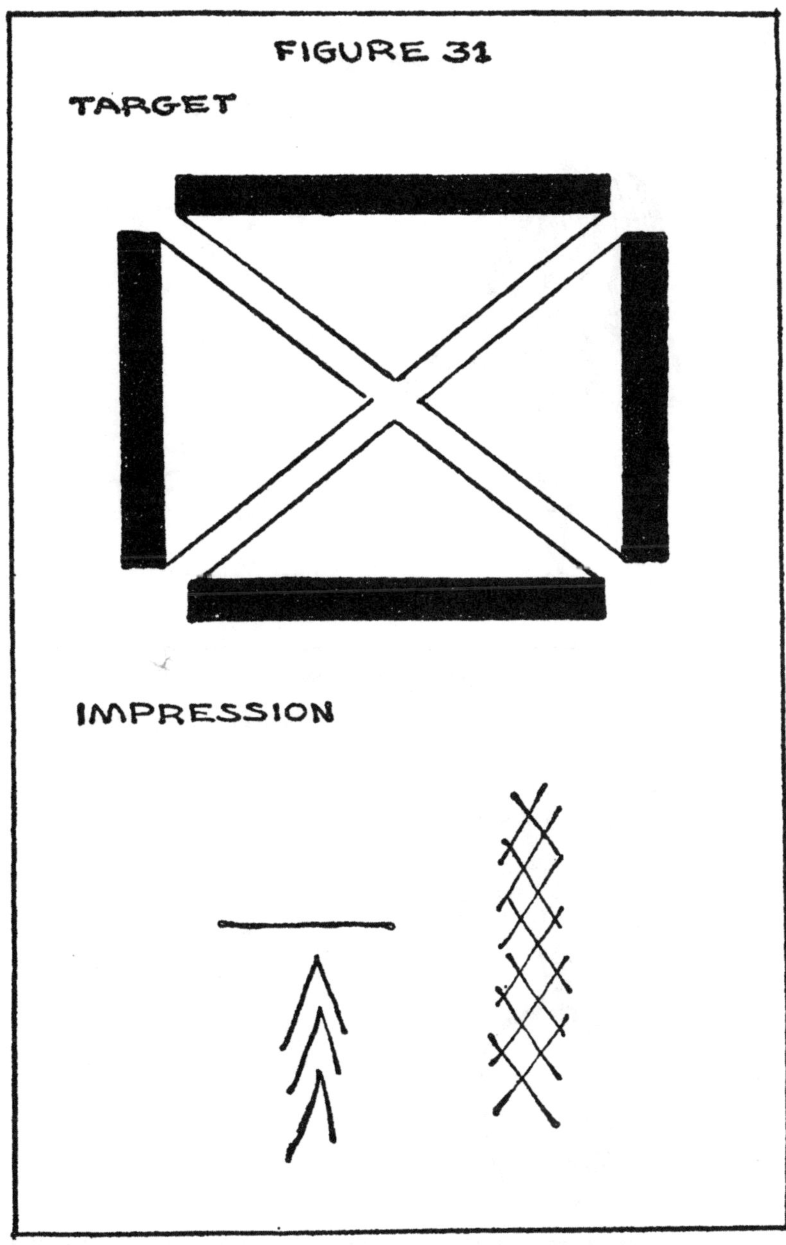

There is no metaphysical implication in the material I am presenting here. Our experiments are empirical and the data are presented as objective facts. I have made no compromise with my critical faculties. The parapsychologist does not wish to leave the impression that the mental image exists in objective

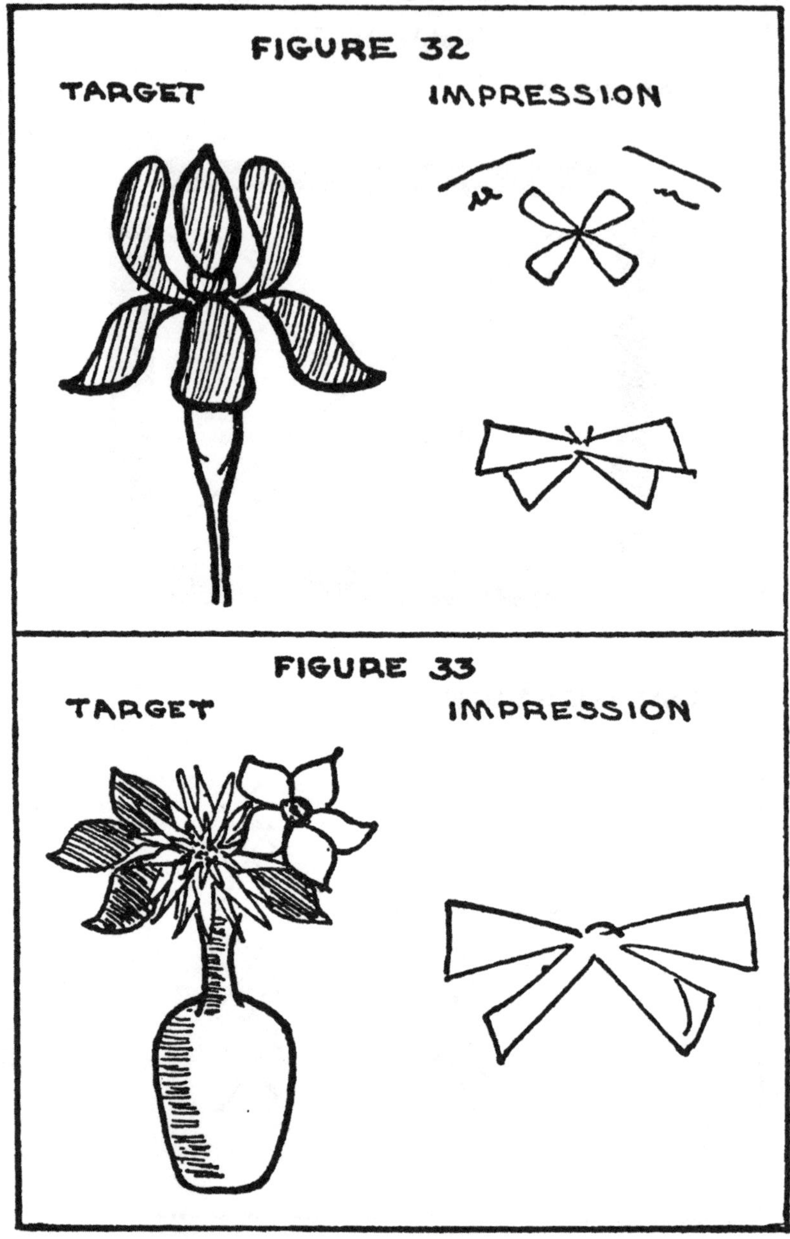

space. It may be purely a fiction, but it is a scientifically necessary one. If it has reality, it is a psychological reality. Its existence lies in its function, which is never independent of the personalities involved. What is more, it is accessible to experimental investigation.

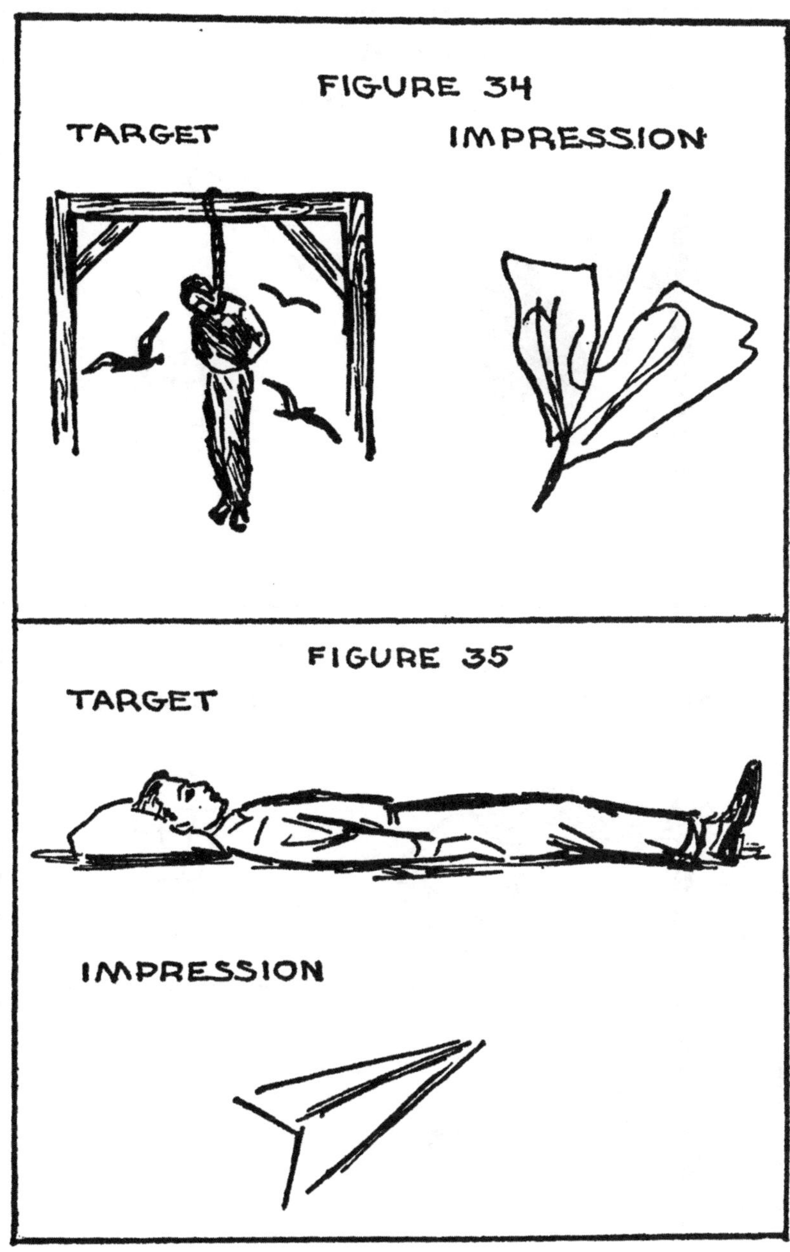

Human psychology is still in its infancy. There is much to be learned about the structure of the personality and about those forces to which we apply so glibly the term "human nature." Research in telepathy will have meaning in enlarging the horizons of psychological investigators. I have been able to point

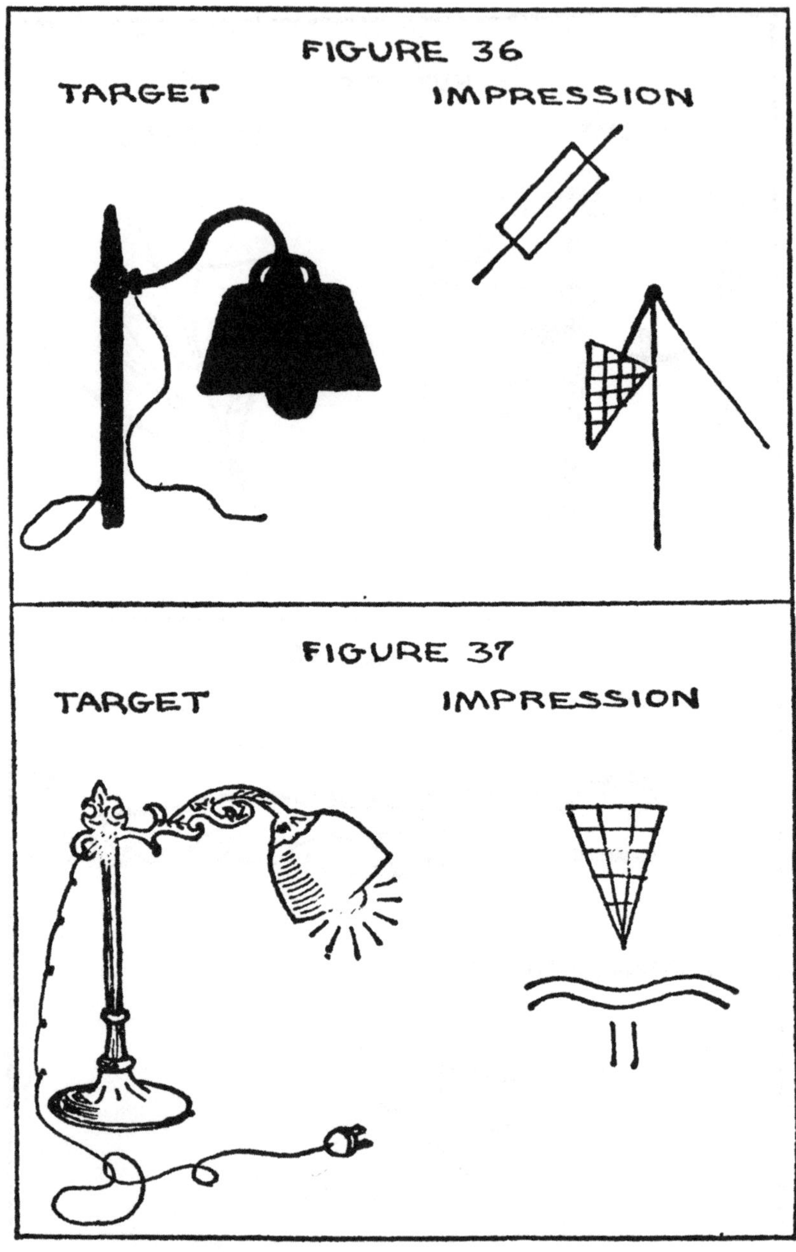

out a few of the psychological principles that seem to apply to telepathy. Moreover, the normal psychology of perception can benefit from suggestions gleaned from telepathic studies. Tactile and kinesthetic elements, for example, seem to play large roles in mental imagery, and Gestalt theoretical principles involving quanta of form may require elaboration to include quanta of movement. At this point, it is appropriate to recall what McDougall had to say concerning the value of parapsychology. He said, "I believe that telepathy is very nearly established for all time among the facts recognised by Science. . . . If and when that result shall have been achieved, its importance for Science and Philosophy will far outweigh the sum of the achievements of all the psychological laboratories of the universities of two continents."[8]

Behaviorists and other mechanistic psychologists have maintained that thought is an imponderable, whether its source is internal or external, and that introspection has little or no value. They hold that psychological experience, that is, personal experience, is no proof of the existence of thought or states of mind. Orthodox psychology, it would seem, might be advanced if it concerned itself with the methods and findings of parapsychology. Thought and states of mind are as real as electrons. The use of introspection in clinical psychology and psychiatry is not considered fantastic. Its practical effectiveness in helping the psychotherapist understand the dynamics of personality has been amply demonstrated. The entire problem of transference and counter-transference in a psychoanalytic sense is involved with the question of telepathy.

Orthodox psychology has resisted the investigation of those very experiences that it seeks to eliminate arbitrarily from its scope. Watson's statement is typical of this whole group of so-called scientists. He said, "It is a serious misunderstanding of the behavioristic position to say . . . 'and of course a behaviorist does not deny that mental states exist. He merely prefers to ignore them.' He 'ignores' them in the same sense that chemistry ignores alchemy, astronomy horoscopy, and psychology telepathy and psychic manifestations. The behaviorist does not concern himself with them because, as the stream of his science broadens and deepens, such old concepts are sucked under, never to reappear."[9]

Mechanistic psychologists, biologists, and physicists have used this offense as a defense against dealing with the paranormal about which they are not adequately informed. They have revealed their position as scientists who have limited their effectiveness and understanding of human nature because of an *a priori* denial of the facts of parapsychology. Fortunately, the list of scientists who are giving time and energy to a consideration and a study of the paranormal is becoming steadily longer and more impressive. Moreover, chemistry no longer ignores alchemy; neither does nuclear physics. Alchemy was rejuvenated by the dramatic transmutation of metals with the fission of uranium atom 235. We have yet to penetrate the secrets of the mind.

GLOSSARY

Agent, sender or source of telepathic impulse or message; in experimental situations, the experimenter or the one who looks at the target, as contrasted with the subject or receiver; opposite of *percipient.*

Analysis, disintegration of an image into fragments without regard for its manifest elements; sometimes called *fragmentation.* See *dissociation.*

Association, process of linking images, perceptions, feelings or ideas.

Automatism, an expressive act performed without volition, such as *automatic writing.*

Clairvoyance, perception of an external object or event without the help of the ordinary senses and, in contradistinction to telepathy, without the use of another mind or agent. See *extrasensory perception* and *telepathy.*

Condensation, fusing of several impressions so that the resulting composite or contamination is representative or symbolic; opposite of *multiplication.*

Dermographism, a condition in which pressure or friction on the skin gives rise to a raised area so that a word traced on it becomes visible.

Dissociation, orderly decomposition or separation into component parts of an image; opposite of *synthesis.* See *analysis.*

Dream, sequence of images perceived during sleep.

Eidetic Image, an unusually vivid and life-like image that remains after the perceived object has been removed; a primary memory image of more permanent character than an after-image; often has some components of activity or movement; most frequently found among children.

Extrasensory Perception (ESP), knowledge gained from or about another person or an external object without the help of the ordinary senses; includes *telepathy* and *clairvoyance.*

Fragmentation, see *analysis.*

Free Association, free-flowing, unselected chain of associations.

Gestalt, (1) configuration or form; (2) the name of a systematic set of principles applied also to human behavior. *Gestalt Psychology* emphasizes the wholeness or organismic character of human behavior.

Global, term used to describe an image, perception or process that is very primitive and highly undifferentiated. See *syncretism.*

Hypnosis, induced sleep-like state of hypersuggestibility accompanied by narrowing of the range of attention.

Image, reproduction of previous perceptual experience in the absence of the actual stimulus.

Impression, vague experience, judgment or feeling in reaction to stimulation.

Introspection, conscious focusing of the attention inward, that is, upon subjective ideas, feelings or impressions.

Inversion, reversal of figure and ground; shift of some characteristics from the background to the foreground, and the reverse; used here to mean a kind of *analysis.*

Latency, time lag between the transmission and the awareness of a telepathic impression.

Mental Contagion, spread of impressions, with or without alteration, from mind to mind; under experimental conditions, a collective sharing of a paranormal perception.

Metagnome, especially sensitive percipient of telepathic or other paranormal impressions.

Movement, dynamic quality of images, perceptions or other organized psychological processes that are under tension; implies activity.

Multiplication, introduction of associated ideas or feelings to elaborate a simple impression; related to *reduplication;* opposite of *condensation.* See *parallelism.*

Parallelism, tendency of similar telepathic impressions or fragments to nest or group according to similarity.

Paranormal, psychic; related to parapsychology.

Parapsychology, that part of the science of behavior of organisms which deals especially with *psychic phenomena.*

Perception, awareness of external or internal stimulation; process of recognizing the meaning of an *impression.*

Percipient, receiver of telepathic impulse or message; opposite of *agent.*

Prägnanz, principle of *Gestalt* theory that all organized processes tend to be as good or complete as possible.

Precognition, non-inferential foreknowledge; correct awareness of future events that cannot be deduced from normally known data in the present.

Psychiatry, branch of medicine dealing with the diagnosis and treatment of mental disorders and disturbances; *medical psychology.*

Psychic Phenomena (Psi), parapsychological processes; such as, *extrasensory perception, psychokinesis, precognition.*

Psychical Research, systematic study, by qualitative and quantitative methods, of borderline happenings in human behavior; includes within its scope all *psychic phenomena.*

Psychoanalysis, body of psychological doctrines and therapeutic techniques using free association, dreams and blunders to reveal unconscious mechanisms and conflicts.

Psychokinesis (PK), direct influence of the mind upon a physical object or event without the help of any known physical energy; also known as *telekinesis.*

Psychology, science of the behavior of organisms.

Psychometry, paranormal acquisition of information by contact with an object and *free association.*

Psychopathology, body of knowledge concerning the cause and nature of mental disease.

Reduplication, see *multiplication.*

Rorschach Technique, method of personality analysis in which responses of the subject to ten ambiguous ink blots are studied.

Schema, unconscious bodily adjustments to afferent impulses.

Subject, individual participating in an experiment; in telepathic research either *agent* or *percipient.*

Syncretism, tendency to gain a total impression without differentiating the parts or distinguishing the details. See *global.*

Synthesis, reconstruction of a whole image from fragments or parts; opposite of *dissociation.*

Tachistoscope, laboratory apparatus equipped with timing device and speed shutter for controlling very brief exposure of images.

Target, image or object used as message or stimulus in *telepathy, clairvoyance* or *psychokinesis.*

Telepathy, communication from one mind to another or to many others without the help of known sensory data; an awareness of how another person is feeling or what he is thinking gained directly without the use of the ordinary senses.

Waking State, opposite of trance or sleep state.

NOTES

All authors mentioned below are included in the Bibliography.

Frame of Reference

1. The earliest systematic investigations of telepathy were largely studies of spontaneous cases; for example, those of Gurney, Podmore and Myers. Spontaneous occurrences of telepathy are not predictable or repeatable. Moreover, they commonly give rise to many questions of testimony and evidence. They have the advantage, nonetheless, of appearing in a life-context. They are, therefore, rich in motivation and interpersonal implication. More recently, psychical research workers have turned more and more to the laboratory; for example, Bruck, Carington, Rhine and his associates. They wish to study the manifestations of the paranormal ability under rigidly defined conditions and under controls of time, place, and meaning. They claim in this way to seek indisputable evidence—generally of a quantitative kind—and to establish a repeatable crucial experiment. They want to get "proof" of the existence of telepathy and to be able better to understand the dynamics, that is, the forces involved. On the other hand, those who emphasize the spontaneous material claim that experimental conditions militate against the appearance of telepathic phenomena. The experimentalists respond by varying the conditions so as to provide for many dynamic factors.

2. The relationship between the occurrence of telepathy and sleep is extremely suggestive but obscure. Telepathic dreams have stimulated the interest of psychoanalysts, such as Ehrenwald and Eisenbud. Some experiments have been conducted under conditions approximating sleep, such as trance-like states of dissociation, and hypnotic states induced by suggestion and drugs; for example, the work of Bruck, Grela, and Rhine. A discussion of the problem of relaxation and telepathy may be found in the paper by Murphy and Dale.

3. The use of drawings in experiments in paranormal cognition complicates the study considerably. It becomes almost impossible to isolate telepathy from clairvoyance. When the

experiment allows either telepathy or clairvoyance, or both, to appear, the term, "General Extrasensory Perception (GESP)," is used by Rhine and others. Carington, Hettinger, Sinclair, Stuart, Taves, Murphy and Dale, and Tischner have also used drawings as targets.

4. The seeming unimportance of distance in paranormal perception is most clearly apparent in spontaneous cases. There is evidence also in the experimental work of Carington, Hettinger, Pratt and others at Duke University, that this may be so.

5. Warcollier, in one of his studies, discusses eidetic imagery as a form of paranormal perception. Eidetic imagery is an area which may continue to yield fruitful results; pioneering work has been done by Allport, Jaensch, Klüver, and Zeman.

6. The Warcollier illustrations are copies of the originals, which are in the possession of the Editor.

Parallelism

1. Figures 4, 5, and 6 are from Upton Sinclair, *Mental Radio,* p. 91, p. 149, and p. 152, respectively. Figure 7 is from Usher and Burt, *Thought Transference,* pp. 586 and 594.

Latency

1. Time orientation is an important theoretical consideration in parapsychology. Dunne, Rhine, Soal, and Goldney have applied themselves to this problem especially in relation to precognition. A discussion of precognition and retrocognition may be found in the recent article by Gardner Murphy, "An Approach to Precognition," *J. A.S.P.R.,* XLII (1948), 3-14.

2. The statement by Barrington-Emerson appears in "Deux mises à l'épreuve de la Connaissance paranormale de M. Stephen Ossowiecki," *Revue Métapsychique,* 1929, No. 1, p. 25 f.

3. The evaluation of Forthuny by Moutier may be found in "Étude critique d'une voyance de M. Pascal Forthuny," *Revue Métapsychique,* 1935, No. 2, p. 140.

Dissociation

1. Figure 10 is from Upton Sinclair, *Mental Radio,* p. 159.

2. The mechanisms of psychopathology and of telepathy seem to have many parallels. The new work by Jan Ehrenwald, *Telepathy and Medical Psychology,* New York: W. W. Norton, 1948, is devoted to this very problem. In this connection there is much to be gained from a study of the works of Eisenbud, Freud, Murphy, Pederson-Krag, Reeves, Rhine, and Tyrrell.

Analysis

1. Figure 12 is from Upton Sinclair, *Mental Radio,* p. 144.

2. Figure 13 is from René Warcollier, *Experimental Telepathy,* p. 257 f.

Synthesis

1. Concentration and relaxation are discussed in the note to page 4.

Syncretism

1. Gertrude Dworetzki, "Le Test de Rorschach," p. 287.

Movement

1. The discussion of the case of the fan as well as Figure 19 may be found in René Warcollier, *Experimental Telepathy,* p. 39.

2. Roger Cousinet, "Un caractère de la perception enfantine," p. 51.

3. Lipps is quoted in Karl Bühler, *Die Gestaltwahrnehmungen.*

4. The discussion of targets, especially those involving movement, is supplemented in René Warcollier, *Experimental Telepathy,* pp. 64-68.

Prägnanz

1. Gestalt theory and Gestalt psychology are especially valuable as points of approach to problems of perception. Koffka's work is basic in this connection.

Emotional Factors

1. The question of personality structure, types, needs, and forces is fundamental to any study of telepathy. All too little work has been done in attempting to analyze the personality factors that facilitate or impede telepathic reception. Some work however has been done in this area by Ehrenwald, Humphrey, Murphy, Pegram (Reeves), Rhine, Schmeidler, and Tyrrell.

2. Upton Sinclair, *Menial Radio,* Chapter XII, pp. 95-103.

3. The role of color in the target is discussed at greater length by Warcollier in his *Experimental Telepathy,* pp. 36-37; 149-151.

Imagination

1. The statement concerning the relationship between percipient and agent is from C. E. Stuart, "GESP Experiments with the Free Response Method," p. 21.

Telepathy and Language

1. It is conceivable that future study will reveal a striking parallel between a telepathic message and a dream. Warcollier stresses the point throughout this work as well as his other writings. It may not be going too far at this time to suggest the possibility that there exists latent as well as manifest content in a telepathic communication, and that the manifest content suffers all the distortion and disguise found in dreams. Concerning this

process called dream work, which may have its counterpart in the working over of a telepathic message before it comes into awareness, the reader is referred to the works of Eisenbud, Ellis, Freud, and other writers in the field of psychoanalysis.

2. The statement by Nolan D. C. Lewis may be found in Margaret Naumberg, "Studies of the 'Free' Art Expression of Behavior Problem Children and Adolescents," p. vi.

3. Many questions concerning the origin of speech in man are raised by studies in telepathy. Attention is focused on the early stages of development of language as seen in the study of primitive language, and of the language of children and psychotics. A more important set of theoretical considerations is raised in relation to communication in pre-linguistic stages, not only between mother and infant, and perhaps even mother and fetus, but also communication between organisms before 'speaking man,' from a phylogenetic standpoint. See the works of Blondel, Ehrenwald, Goldstein, Janet, Kasanin, Lévy-Bruhl, Montmasson, and Tyrrell.

4. G. N. M. Tyrrell, "Presidential Address," p. 308.

Telepathy and Thought

1. Bergson, *L'Energie Spirituelle,* (Alcan, p. 138); R. Warcollier, *La Télépathie* (Alcan, p. 40); *Revue Métapsychique,* No. 4, 1929, pp. 275-277.

2. Abramowski, *Le Subconscient normal (Télépathie expérimentale) and Journal de Psychologie normale et pathologique,* Année IX, No. 6, Nov.-Dec., 1912.

3. William Friedrich, *Experimental Psychologie und experimental Metaphysik,* Leipzig, 1891, pp, 60-63.

4. Teste, *Manuel pratique de Magnétisme animal,* Ballière, 1846, p. 137.

5. Paris, *Traité du Somnanbulisme,* Dentu, 1823, p. 739.

6. Louis Figuier, "Les diables de Loudun," *Histoire du Merveilleux,* Tome I, Hachette, 1860.

7. Dr. Ochorowicz, *La Suggestion Mentale,* Doin, 1889, p. 257.

8. Ch. Lafontaine, *L'Art de Magnétiser,* Alcan, 1899, p. 238.

9. "Télépathie spontanée et Transmission de pensée expérimentale," *Revue Métapsychique,* 1932 and 1933.

10. Ley and Wauthier, "Études sur l'imagination," *Journal de Psychologie normale et pathologique,* Alcan, Juillet-Décembre, 1939.

11. Titchener, *Manuel de Psychologie,* Alcan, p. 534.

12. V. Panfilov, "À propos de rapports entre la langue et la pensée," *Linguistique,* Recherches Internationales, No. 7, Mai, Juin, 1958, Les Editions de la Nouvelle Critique, Paris.

13. R. Pellet, *Essai d'analyse de la pensée chez l'enfant sourdmuet,* Bosc et Rion, Lyon, 1938. See also Pierre Oléron, "Recherches sur le développement mental des Sourds-Muets," Contribution à l'étude du probleme "Langage et Pensée."

14. R. Warcollier, "La Télépathie et l'Imagination," R.M., 1930, p. 323.

15. Ribot, "Essais sur l'Imagination créatrice," Alcan, p. 22.

16. Pierre Janet, *Journal de Psychologie,* 15 Janv.-15 Mars, 1921, XXIe Année, No. 1-3, p. 161.

17. Lire, "Les Signes et le Langage," *Leçons de philosophie de D. Roustan,* Delagrave, 1923, p. 454.

18. C. Konczewski, "La Pensée Préconsciente," *Incubation subconsciente,* Alcan, pp. 45, 52-53.

19. "A Marked Case of Mimetic Ideation," *Psychologic Review,* XVII, 1910, pp. 239-243.

20. M. Rowland, *Psychological Review,* 1907, Sup. 32.

21. E. Lubac, *Les Niveaux de Conscience et l'Inconscient et Leurs Communications,* Alcan, 1920.

22. R. M. Déc., 1957, No. 6 (Note to page 51).

23. "Psychologie," *Leçons de Philosophie de D. Roustan,* Delagrave, Chapter 1.

Conclusion

1. An analysis of the resistances to the study and investigation of psychical phenomena is to be found in G. N. M. Tyrrell, *The Personality of Man,* Chapters 26-30.

2. The statement is from Whately Carington, "Experiments on the Paranormal Cognition of Drawings, III," p. 106.

3. Further material on pertinent theoretical considerations in physiological psychology may be found in Banerji, Ehrenwald, Goldstein and Koffka.

4. Hettinger's experiments in "psychometric telepathy" are worthy of attention in connection with the entire problem of telepathy, clairvoyance, general extrasensory perception, and psychometry.

5. Upton Sinclair, *Mental Radio,* pp. 178-203.

6. The reader must be aware of the fact that Warcollier does not include in this work his criteria for evaluating the success of an experiment. It is known from other sources that he has developed a "weighting technique" for this purpose. For a description of reliable and valid methods for evaluating responses in telepathic experiments employing drawings, see the works of Carington and Stuart.

7. For a fuller account of mental contagion, see René Warcollier, *Experimental Telepathy,* pp. 76-81; 240-244. For a discussion of collective hallucinations, see the works of Gurney, Myers, and Podmore, and of Tyrrell.

8. William McDougall, "Presidential Address," p. 109.

9. John B. Watson, "Is Thinking Merely the Action of Language Mechanisms?" p. 94.

E. K. S.

I BIBLIOGRAPHY

Abramowski, E. *Le Subconscient normal.* Paris: Alcan, 1914.

Allport, G. W. "Eidetic Imagery," *Brit. J. Psychol.,* XV (1924), 99-120.

Angier, R. P., Cobb, P. W., Dallenbach, K. M., Dunlap, K., Fernberger, S. W., Johnson, H. M, and McComas H. C. "Adequate Experimental Testing of the Hypothesis of 'Extra-Sensory Perception' Based on Card-Sorting," *J. Parapsychol.,* III (1939), 29-37.

Banerji, M. N. "Synaesthesia," *Indian J. Psychol.,* 5 (1930), 147-159.

Bergson, H. *Matter and Memory.* London: George Allen and Unwin Ltd., 1929.

Besterman, T. "An Experiment in 'Clairvoyance' with M. Stefan Ossowiecki," *Proc. S.P.R.,* XLI (1933), 345-351.

Binet-Sanglé, C. *La Fin du Secret.* Paris: Albion Michel, 1922.

Blondel, C. *La Mentalité Primitive.* Paris: Stock, 1926.

Bruck, C. *Experimentelle Telepathie.* Stuttgart: Julius Püttmann Verlag, 1925.

Bühler, K. *Die Gestaltwahrnehmungen.* Stuttgart: 1913.

Carington, W. "Experiments on the Paranormal Cognition of Drawings, III. Steps in the Development of a Repeatable Technique," *Proc. A.S.P.R.,* XXIV (1944), 1-107.

Carington, W., "Experiments on the Paranormal Cognition of Drawings, IV," *Proc. S.P.R.,* XLVII (1944), 155-228.

Carington, W. *Thought Transference: An Outline of Facts, Theory and Implications of Telepathy.* New York: Creative Age Press, Inc., 1946.

Claparède, E. *L'Association des Idées.* Paris: Doin, 1903.

Claparède, E. "A Propos d'un Cas de Perception Syncrétique," *Arch. de Psychol.,* XXVI (1938), 367-377.

Cousinet, R. "Un caractère de la perception enfantine," *La Nouvelle Education,* XI (1932), 49-52.

Cousinet, R. *Une méthode de travail libre par groupes.* Paris: Cerf, 1945.

DeLacroix, H. *Les Grandes Formes de la Vie Mentale.* Paris: Alcan, 1937.

Driesch, H. *Psychical Research.* London: G. Bell and Sons, 1933.

Dunne, J. W. *An Experiment with Time.* New York: The Macmillan Company, 1927.

Dworetzki, G. "Le Test de Rorschach et L'Évolution de la Perception Étude Experimentale," *Arch. de Psychol.,* XXVII (1939), 233-396.

Ehrenwald, J. "Psychopathological Aspects of Telepathy," *Proc. S.P.R.,* XLVI (1941), 224-244.

Ehrenwald, J. "Exploring Telepathy: An Inquiry into Method." *J. A.S.P.R.,* XLI (1947) pp. 145-154.

Eisenbud, J. "Telepathy and Problems of Psychoanalysis," *Psychoanal. Quart.,* XV (1946), 32-87.

Eisenbud, J. "The Dreams of Two Patients in Analysis Interpreted as a Telepathic *Rêve à Deux," Psychoanal. Quart.,* XVI (1947), 39-60.

Ellis, H. *The World of Dreams.* Boston: Houghton Mifflin Company, 1926.

Eng, H. The Psychology of Children's Drawings. New York: Harcourt, Brace and Company, 1931.

Freud, S. *New Introductory Lectures on Psycho-Analysis.* New York: W. W. Norton, 1933.

Freud, S. *The Basic Writings of Sigmund Freud.* New York: The Modern Library, 1938.

Garrett, E. J. *Telepathy.* New York: Creative Age Press, Inc., 1941.

Goldstein, K. *The Organism.* New York: American Book Company, 1939.

Greenwood, J. A., and Stuart, C. E. "Mathematical Techniques Used in ESP Research," *J. Parapsychol.,* I (1937), 206-225.

Grela, J. J. "Effect on ESP Scoring of Hypnotically Induced Attitudes," *J. Parapsychol.,* IX (1945), 194-202.

Guillaume, P. *La Psychologie de la Forme.* Paris: Flammarion, 1942.

Gurney, E., Myers, F. W. H., and Podmore, F. *Phantasms of the Living.* London: Trübner and Company, 2 vols., 1886.

Hettinger, J. *The Ultra-Perceptive Faculty.* London: Rider and Company, 1940.

Hettinger, J. *Exploring the Ultra-Perceptive Faculty.* London: Rider and Company, 1941.

Hettinger, J. "Psychometric Telepathy Across the Atlantic," *J. A.S.P.R.,* XLI (1947), 94-122.

Humphrey, B. M. "Patterns of Success in an ESP Experiment," *J. Parapsychol.,* VII (1943), 5-19.

Jaensch, E. R. *Eidetic Imagery.* New York: Harcourt, Brace and Company, 1930.

Janet, P. *Les débuts de l'intelligence.* Paris: Flammarion, 1935.

Janet, P. *L'Intelligence avant le langage.* Paris: Flammarion, 1936.

Jorres, J. von. "La Mystique Divine," in *Poussielgue de 1882.* Paris.

Kasanin, J. S. *Language and Thought in Schizophrenia.* Berkeley: University of California Press, 1946.

Kennedy, J. L. "A Methodological Review of Extra-Sensory Perception," *Psychol. Bull.,* XXXVI (1939), 59-103.

Klüver, H. "An Experimental Study of the Eidetic Type," *Genet. Psychol. Mon.,* I (1926), 71-230.

Klüver, H. "Fragmentary Eidetic Imagery," *Psychol. Rev.,* XXXVII (1930), 441-458.

Koffka, K. *Principles of Gestalt Psychology.* New York: Harcourt, Brace and Company, 1935.

Konczewski, C. *La Pensée Préconsciente.* Paris: Alcan, 1939.

Lévy-Bruhl, L. *Les Fonctions Mentales dans Les Sociétés Inférieures.* Paris: Alcan, 1910.

McDougall, W. "Presidential Address," *Proc. S.P.R.,* XXXI (1920-1), 105-123.

Mead, G. H. *Mind, Self and Society.* Chicago: University of Chicago Press, 1934.

Monmasson, J. M. *Invention and the Unconscious.* New York: Harcourt, Brace and Company, 1932.

Murphy, G. "Parapsychology," in Harriman, P. L. *Encyclopedia of Psychology.* New York: Philosophical Library, 1946, 417-436.

Murphy, G. "Psychical Phenomena and Human Needs." *J. A.S.P.R.,* XXXVII (1943), 163-191.

Murphy, G., and Dale, L. A. "Concentration Versus Relaxation in Relation to Telepathy." *J. A.S.P.R.,* XXXVII (1943), 2-15.

Murphy, G., and Taves, E. "Covariance Methods in the Comparison of Extra-Sensory Tasks," *J. Parapsychol.,* III (1939), 38-78.

Myers, F. W. H. *Human Personality and Its Survival of Bodily Death.* London: Longmans, Green, and Company, 2 vols., 1903.

Naumberg, M. "Studies of the 'Free' Art Expression of Behavior Problem Children and Adolescents as a Means of Diagnosis and Therapy," *Nervous and Mental Disease Monographs No. 71.* New York: 1947.

Pederson-Krag, G. "Telepathy and Repression," *Psychoanal. Quart.,* XVI (1947), 61-68.

Pegram, M. H. "Some Psychological Relations of Extra-Sensory Perception," *J. Parapsychol.,* 1 (1937), 191-205.

Philippe, Y. *L'Image Mentale.* Paris: Alcan, 1903.

Piéron, Henri. *Thought and the Brain.* New York: Harcourt, Brace and Company, 1921.

Pratt, J. G. "A Further Advance in Methods of Testing Extra-Sensory Perception," *J. Parapsychol.,* III (1939), 95-100.

Pratt, J. G., Rhine, J. B., Smith, B. M., Stuart, C. E., and Greenwood, J. A. *Extra-Sensory Perception After Sixty Years.* New York: Henry Holt and Company, 1940.

Pratt, J. G., and Woodruff, J. L. "Size of Stimulus Symbols in Extra-Sensory Perception," *J. Parapsychol.,* III (1939), 121-158.

Price, H. H. *Perception.* London: Methuen and Company, 1932.

Prince, W. F. "The Sinclair Experiments Demonstrating Telepathy," *Bulletin XVI* (1932), Boston S.P.R.

Reeves, M. P. (Pegram) "A Topological Approach to Parapsychology," *J. A.S.P.R.,* XXXVIII (1944), 72-82.

Rhine, J. B. *Extra-Sensory Perception.* Boston: Bruce Humphries, 1934.

Rhine, J. B. *New Frontiers of the Mind.* New York: Farrar and Rinehart, 1937.

Rhine, J. B. "Some Basic Experiments in Extra-Sensory Perception: A Background," *J. Parapsychol.,* I (1937), 70-80.

Rhine, J. B. *The Reach of the Mind.* New York: William Sloane Associates, 1947.

Richet, C. *Thirty Years of Psychical Research.* New York: The Macmillan Company, 1923.

Rorschach, H. *Psychodiagnostics.* Berne: Verlag Hans Huber, 1942.

Sartre, J. P. *Esquisse d'une théorie des émotions.* Paris: Hermann, 1939.

Schmeidler, G. R. "Rorschach Variables in Relation to ESP Scores," *J. A.S.P.R.,* XLI (1947), 35-64.

Schmeidler, G. R., and Murphy, G. "The Influence of Belief and Disbelief in ESP upon Individual Scoring Levels," *J. Exp. Psychol.,* XXXVI (1946), 271-276.

Schmoll, A. "Experiments in Thought-Transference," *Proc. S.P.R.,* IV (1887), 324-337.

Schmoll, A., and Mabire, J. E. "Experiments in Thought-Transference," *Proc. S.P.R.,* V (1989), 169-207.

Sherif, M., and Cantril, H. *The Psychology of Ego-Involvements.* New York: John Wiley & Sons, Inc., 1947.

Sinclair, Upton. *Mental Radio.* Pasadena: Upton Sinclair, 1930.

Soal, S. G. "Experiments in Supernormal Perception at a Distance," *Proc. S.P.R.,* XL (1932), 165-362.

Soal, S. G. "Fresh Light on Card Guessing—Some New Effects," *Proc. S.P.R.,* XLVI (1940), 152-198.

Soal, S. G., and Goldney, K. M. "Experiments in Precognitive Telepathy," *Proc. S.P.R.,* XLVII (1943), 21-150.

Stuart, C. E. "An ESP Test with Drawings," *J. Parapsychol.,* VI (1942), 20-43.

Stuart, C. E. "GESP Experiments with the Free Response Method," *J. Parapsychol.,* X (1946), 21-35.

Stuart, C. E., and Pratt, J. G. *A Handbook for Testing Extra-Sensory Perception.* New York: Farrar and Rinehart, 1937.

Taves, E., Murphy, G., and Dale, L. A. "American Experiments on the Paranormal Cognition of Drawings," *J. A.S.P.R.,* XXXIX (1945), 144-150,

Taylor, G. Le M. "Experimental Comparison between Chance and Thought-Transference in Correspondence of Diagrams," *Proc. S.P.R.,* VI (1890), 398-405.

Thouless, R. H. "Report on Glasgow Repetition of Dr. Rhine's Experiments on Extra-Sensory Perception," *Proc. S.P.R.,* XLV (1939), 252-256.

Tischner, R. *Telepathy and Clairvoyance.* New York: Harcourt, Brace and Company, 1925.

Tyrrell, G. N. M. "Further Research in Extra-Sensory Perception," *Proc. S.P.R.,* XLIV (1937), 99-167.

Tyrrell, G. N, M. *Science and Psychical Phenomena.* New York: Harper and Brothers, 1939.

Tyrrell, G. N. M. *Apparitions, Being the Seventh Frederic W. M. Myers Memorial Lecture.* London: Society for Psychical Research, 1942.

Tyrrell, G. N. M., "Presidential Address," *Proc. S.P.R.,* XLVII (1942-5), 301-319.

Tyrrell, G. N. M. *The Personality of Man.* Harmondsworth, Middlesex, England: Penguin Books, 1946.

Usher, F. L., and Burt, F. P. "Thought Transference," *Annals Psychic. Sci.,* VIII (1909), 561-600.

Warcollier, R. *La Télépathie.* Paris: Alcan, 1921.

Warcollier, R. *La Télépathie à très grande distance.* Paris: Terrier Frères et Cie., 1928.

Warcollier, R. "La Télépathie et l'Imagination," *Rev. Métapsych.* (1930), 323-337.

Warcollier, R. *Experimental Telepathy.* Boston: Boston Soc. for Psychic Research, 1938.

Warcollier, R. "Perceptions paranormales et supranormales: l'Eidétisme," *Rev. Métapsych.* (1940), 98-108.

Warcollier, R. "Polyzoisme et Polypsychisme," in *La Métapsychique,* I (1940-1946), 15-72. Paris: Presses Universitaires de France.

Watson, J. B. "Is Thinking Merely the Action of Language Mechanisms?" *Brit. J. Psychol.,* XI (1920), 94.

Woodruff, J. L., and George, R. W. "Experiments in Extra-Sensory Perception," *J. Parapsychol.,* I (1937), 18-30.

Zeman, H. "Die Lehre von der Eidetik und ihre praktische Bedeutung," *Die Quelle,* 79 (1929), 6-17; 171-176.

POSTSCRIPT: TRANSFORMATION OF PSYCHIC IMAGES

Arthur C. Hastings
Professor of psychology, Institute of Transpersonal Psychology

Introduction

One main area of ESP research has been concerned with the telepathic or clairvoyant perception of figures, designs, or pictures. Examples of such studies are Guthrie (1882–84), Sinclair (1930), Warcollier (1948), Musso and Granero (1973), and Targ and Puthoff (1974). In these studies the percipient attempted to reproduce randomly or arbitrarily chosen visual targets. The responses ranged from highly similar reproductions, to partial successes, to responses with no apparent similarity. Recently techniques have been devised to statistically evaluate the results, but as Eisenbud comments, "When a hit occurs—one is intuitively impressed, despite the logical difficulties of critical evaluation." (1970)

We are dealing here, more clearly than in some ESP experiments, with internal, mental images that appear to the mind's eye of the percipient, who then draws or describes them. White (1964), Honorton, Tierney, and Torres (1974) and others have noted that to become aware of internal imagery, percipients usually turn their attention away from the external world and toward their internal thoughts, images, feelings, and memories. This may be done through closing the eyes, sensory deprivation, physical relaxation, and other means. Under these conditions, the percipients seem to be more aware of images stimulated by ESP targets.

Some images reproduced under these conditions are highly accurate, but others are changed, augmented, and modified. I have concluded that these changes are not random, but are the result of mental processing of the internal image. Little is known about how subjective imagery is processed by the mind or brain, but it is presumably similar to the processing of external images. It is thus possible that some ESP imagery is also processed by the internal perceptual system and the percipient's response is the result of his interacting at a perceptual level with the ESP image from the target. This paper will describe several stages in the system of perceptual processing and show how they affect ESP imagery.

Stages of Mental Processing of Visual Perceptions

I will assume that these stages, based on the processing of external perceptions, function also for internal mental images, including internal images derived by extra-sensory perception.

1. *Sense Data.* At the initial stage there are simply impressions without order, composed of lines, colors, forms, shapes, contrasts, extension, etc. There is no overall meaning, only visual display.

2. *Gestalt Organization.* The sense data are then organized into a meaningful pattern, something recognizable. Boundaries are drawn, elements put into relationship, and a perception is formed. In doing this, some theorists have postulated that we develop a stock of semi-independent patterns, or schemata, based on past experience, to organize sensations into perceptions with identity and meaning.

3. *Associations.* Then other memories, experiences, thoughts, ideas, and feelings are activated by the perception. Such associations are made to perceptions subliminally perceived, as well as those noted by conscious attention.

ESP Imagery

Now let us examine how ESP imagery reflects stages of processing in the internal perceptual system, assuming that the target image may either be complete or it may be incomplete as it enters the system.

1. *Unchanged.* Some ESP responses are highly similar or identical to the target image and there seems to be no processing by the internal perceptual system—the ESP image either passes through the system without any change or is presented to conscious awareness without going through the system at all. Any differences between target and reproduction seem plausibly due to

memory, drawing abilities, minor fogging or blurring, just as in external sensory perception. It is as though the ESP image comes in as data and is not modified or interpreted, but simply presented to awareness.

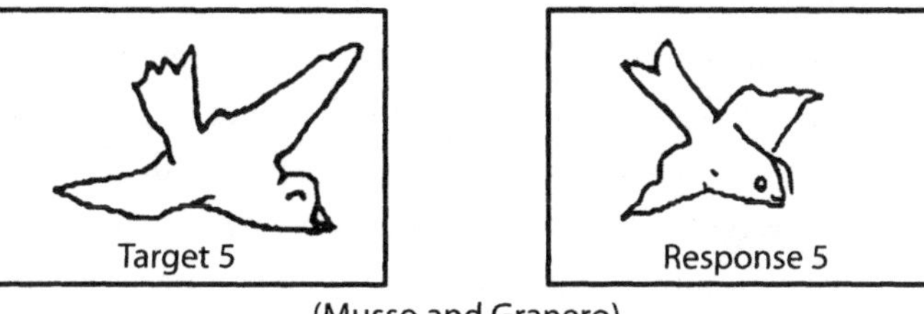

(Musso and Granero)

Sometimes a complete image is seen, but sometimes only a part or some elements are reproduced, as though the sub-units of the image were scanned individually but not put into a gestalt pattern.

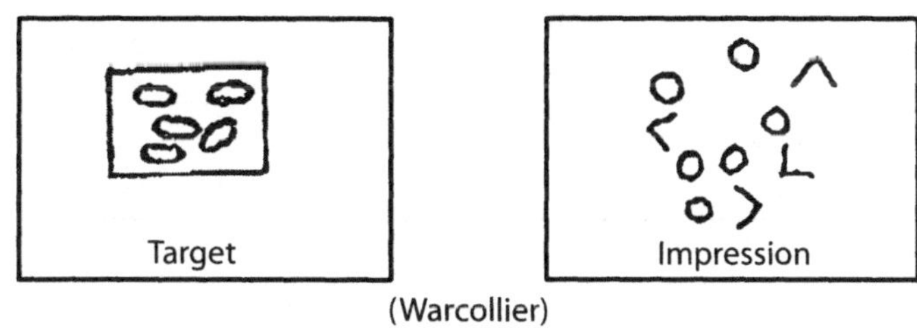

(Warcollier)

2. *Reorganized.* If the target image is presented in parts or elements, these may be reorganized into a pattern or gestalt that creates an identifiable form. The same elements are restructured to make sense, though in a way different from the original configuration. This structural transformation is what Ingo Swann refers to as "analytical overlay."

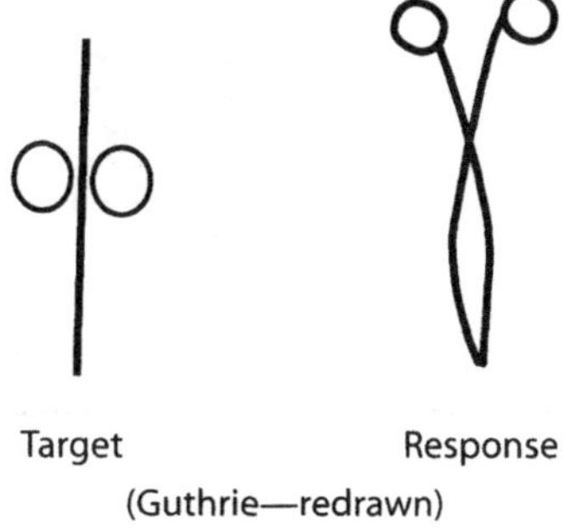

(Guthrie—redrawn)

3. *Embedded Figure.* Here part of the target image is present, but other material has been added, so that the ESP image is embedded in another figure, a different gestalt. This occurs at the stage of Gestalt Organization when the ESP image is incomplete or not a recognizable pattern. A gestalt or pattern is supplied to incorporate the image into a complete, meaningful one, and missing elements are filled in from memory, imagination, and inference. It is as though the process jumps to a conclusion from inadequate evidence and then generates the rest of the evidence necessary to support the conclusion. This type of response is very common and is usually counted as a near-hit, or a near-miss. I prefer to view it as a correct, but partial image, which has been augmented by the percipient's activity at the organization stage of perceptual processing.

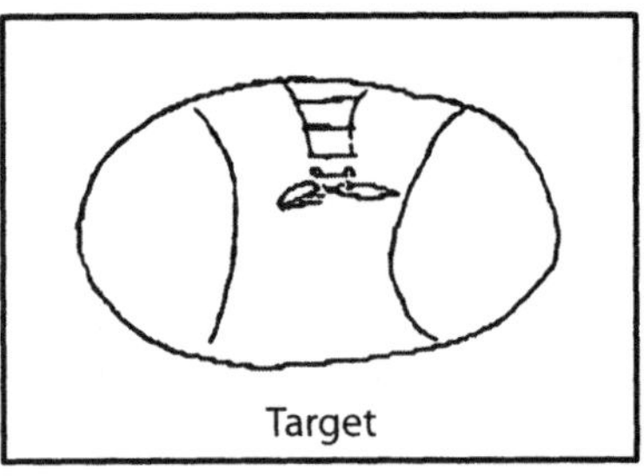
Target

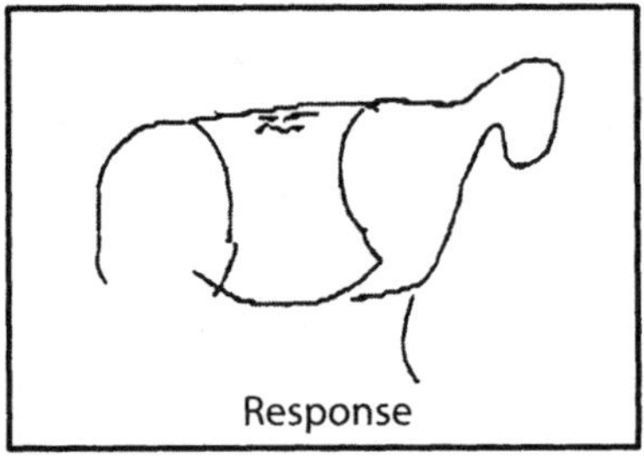
Response

(Sinclair)

4. *Transformation.* This effect is also common. The target image is transformed into a different, but visually similar image. It is as though the original ESP image is blurred or fragmentary, and at the Organization stage of processing, a visually similar figure has been selected and imposed on the image, often overriding it and adding extra data to complete the picture. Thus, the response may be similar in shape but not the same object.

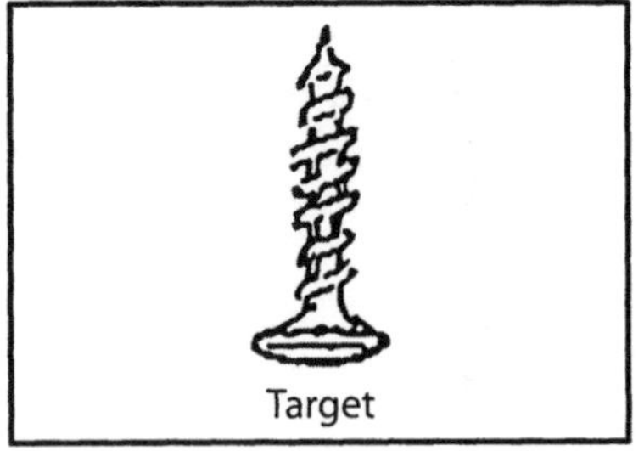
Target

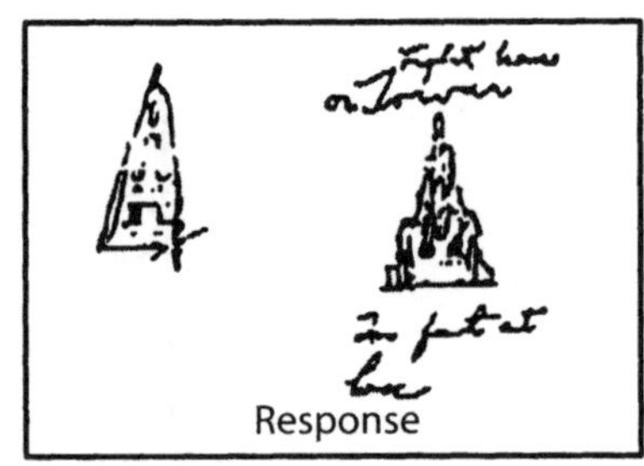
Response

(Sinclair)

5. *Association.* In some cases the ESP image stimulated by the target is not directly seen by the percipient, but it apparently stimulates associations

from memories, ideas, and feelings, and these associated images are reproduced by the percipient. These are similarities in a conceptual or experiential dimension, while the response in #4 is based on visual similarities.

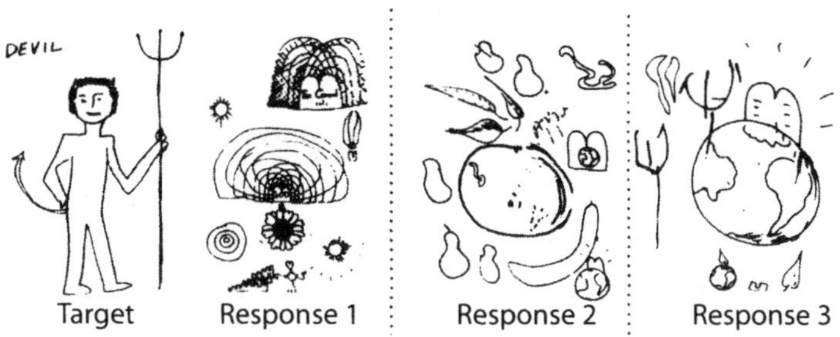

Target Response 1 Response 2 Response 3

Implications

1. In most experiments the reproduced images are evaluated only by their similarity to the targets. I suggest that all these types of processed images be considered responses based on extra-sensory perception. This analysis will give much more information about the operation and functioning of ESP and how it interacts with an individual's internal states and processes.

2. This approach would change the judging task from one in which the question is "Which target is most similar to the response?" to the question "Which target, being mentally processed, would result in this response?"

3. This model enables discrimination among ESP responses in relation to the mental processing of the image. By observing how the ESP image is altered from the target image, the percipient and the experimenter can tell where in the internal perception system the image is being affected, and methods may be devised to keep the image from being manipulated. Percipients can, for example, learn to stay with "sense data" and not unconsciously impose patterns on them or supply gestalts for them. They can learn to relinquish the need to "make sense" of their internal images, or learn to distinguish between the stages of their own mental processing of the images.

4. This model implies that a percipient should not only turn attention away from external sensations and stimuli, but an attempt should also be made to reduce the activity of the internal perception system, and possibly to find ESP imagery that does not come through that system. Perhaps this is the purpose of mental exercises such as imagining a blank screen, holding a

mental image such as a rose, or meditating with the attempt to clear the mind of thoughts. All of these have been used as a way of preparing for ESP imagery (White 1964). Other methods may also be developed, and can be tested by their effects on the image responses.

Final Comment

I have applied this model, specifically to ESP studies involving reproductions of visual images, and I have emphasized the changes in internal ESP images that are caused by the internal perception system. These include visual changes and conceptual experiential associations. It may be that this analysis can be similarly applied to more complicated ESP responses such as dream imagery, verbal descriptions, remote viewing, and thoughtographic picture images.

References

Eisenbud, Jule. *PSI and Psychoanalysis.* New York: Grune and Stratton, 1970.

Guthrie, M. An account of some experiments in thought-transference, *Proc. SPR.* 1884; 2.

Guthrie, M. and Birchall, J. Record of experiments in thought transference, *Proc. SPR.* 1882–3; 1.

Honorton, C., Tierney, L. and Torres, D. The role of mental imagery in psi-mediation, *JASPR.* 1974; 68:4.

Musso, J. R. and Granero, M. An ESP drawing experiment with a high-scoring subject, *J. Parapsychology.* 1973; 37:1.

Sinclair, Upton. *Mental Radio.* New York: Albert and Charles Boni, 1930.

Targ, R. and Puthoff, H. Information transmission under conditions of sensory shielding, *Nature.* 1974; 251.

Warcollier, René. *Mind to Mind.* New York: Creative Age, 1948.

White, Rhea. A comparison of old and new methods of response to targets in ESP experiments, *JASPR.* 1964; 58:1.

Guthrie's experiments are also described in Eisenbud and in *Phantasms of the Living,* by Edmund Gurney, F. W. H. Myers, and Frank Podmore (1962, reprinted edition, New Hyde Park: University Books).

This paper was prepared for the 1975 Parapsychological Association Convention at Santa Barbara, California.

NAME INDEX

SUBJECT INDEX

Hampton Roads Publishing Company

. . . for the evolving human spirit

Hampton Roads Publishing Company
publishes books on a variety of subjects,
including metaphysics, health, integrative medicine,
visionary fiction, and other related topics.

For a copy of our latest catalog, call toll-free
(800) 766-8009, or send your name and address to:

Hampton Roads Publishing Company, Inc.
1125 Stoney Ridge Road
Charlottesville, VA 22902

e-mail: hrpc@hrpub.com
www.hrpub.com